He is the saint of humility, charity, and love for all creatures great and small. He is Francis of Assisi, whose teachings and gentle wisdom have resonated through the ages. In *The Lessons of St. Francis*, John Michael Talbot shows how the life and writings of this beloved thirteenth-century saint can offer us guidance on our paths to greater peace, spirituality, and joy.

Francis turned his back on worldly wealth to embrace the simple virtues: Solitude. Humility. Creativity. Community. Compassion. Service. Prayer. Emulating his joyful meditations and committed practices, we can incorporate the Franciscan philosophy into our daily existence and take meaningful steps toward lives of greater simplicity and deeper spirituality.

The simple words and heartfelt message of St. Francis can touch us in ways we never imagined, affecting the way we live every hour, every day. Practical, down-to-earth, and inspiring, *The Lessons of St. Francis* casts a warm light on the uncertain future, as it guides us along a path that can enhance and transform our lives.

JOHN MICHAEL TALBOT is a musician, teacher, and writer who practices the Franciscan traditions. His albums have sold more than four million copies, and he is the author of a dozen previous books, including *The Lover and the Beloved: A Way of Franciscan Prayer*, *The Fire of God*, and *Meditations from Solitude*. In 1980 he founded Brothers and Sisters of Charity, a monastic community located in Eureka Springs, Arkansas, based on the Franciscan principles of simplicity and self-sufficiency.

STEVE RABEY has written hundreds of articles on religion and spirituality for newspapers and magazines throughout the country. He lives in Colorado Springs.

THE LESSONS OF ST. FRANCIS

How to Bring Simplicity and
Spirituality into Your Daily Life

John Michael Talbot

with Steve Rabey

A PLUME BOOK

PLUME
Published by the Penguin Group
Penguin Putnam Inc., 375 Hudson Street, New York, New York 10014, U.S.A.
Penguin Books Ltd, 27 Wrights Lane, London W8 5TZ, England
Penguin Books Australia Ltd, Ringwood, Victoria, Australia
Penguin Books Canada Ltd, 10 Alcorn Avenue,
Toronto, Ontario, Canada M4V 3B2
Penguin Books (N.Z.) Ltd, 182–190 Wairau Road, Auckland 10, New Zealand

Penguin Books Ltd, Registered Offices: Harmondsworth, Middlesex, England

Published by Plume, an imprint of Dutton NAL, a member of Penguin Putnam Inc.
Previously published in a Dutton edition.

First Plume Printing, October, 1998

20 19 18 17 16 15 14 13 12

Photographs taken at Little Portion Hermitage by John Whitford.

 REGISTERED TRADEMARK—MARCA REGISTRADA

The Library of Congress catalogued the Dutton edition as follows:

Talbot, John Michael.
    The lessons of St. Francis : how to bring simplicity and spirituality into your
    daily life / John Michael Talbot ; with Steve Rabey.
        p.   cm.
    ISBN 0-525-94314-5 (hc.)
    ISBN 0-452-27834-1 (pbk.)
    1. Francis, of Assisi, Saint, 1182–1226.   2. Spiritual life—Catholic Church.
3. Catholic Church—Doctrines.   I. Rabey, Steve,   II. Title.
BX4700.F6T27   1997
271'.302—dc21   97–8709
                                                                            CIP
Printed in the United States of America
Original hardcover design by Leonard Telesca

I would like to dedicate this work to my mother,
Jamie Talbot,
who passed away during its writing
on December 26, 1996.

I would like to thank my spiritual father in the church and Franciscanism, Father Martin Wolter, O.F.M., for his years of support and guidance. I also thank the entire Franciscan family, who include a list of names too long to mention individually, but who grace this work in the Spirit.

Most importantly, I thank my wife, Viola, for her spiritual support in this, and all my work in the community of the Brothers and Sisters of Charity, the church, and the world. In a special way I thank her, and the spiritual family she has helped birth in Christ.

CONTENTS

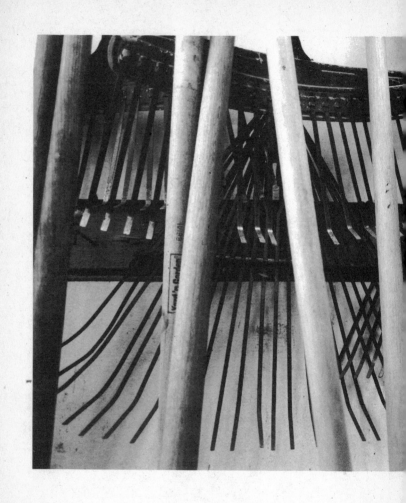

Preach always.
If necessary use words.
                    —FRANCIS

1

A Tangible Saint

❧ *Lord, make me an instrument of your peace.*—PRAYER OF ST. FRANCIS

OURS IS A TIME OF INTENSE spiritual hunger. People are thirsting for the sacred, the mysterious, the mystical. They are looking for more than a good job, a full closet, and a balanced checkbook.

In a sense, this spiritual yearning has flowed like a river throughout human history, at times bubbling under the surface, at other times overflowing its banks as men and women relentlessly pursue spiritual fulfillment. I believe we may be in one of those fiercely spiritual periods.

Perhaps it is no surprise that much of today's spiritual hunger is being met outside of traditional churches and religious institutions. In that way, our day is remarkably similar to a time nearly eight hundred years ago, when a humble man named Francis transformed his world and renewed the church of his day by the simple but revolutionary act of practicing the Christian faith as it had never been practiced before, or since.

> *O how beautiful, how splendid, how glorious did he appear in the innocence of his life, in the simplicity of his words, in the purity of his heart, in his love for God, in his fraternal charity, in his ardent obedience, in his peaceful submission, in his angelic countenance!*—THOMAS OF CELANO

Raised in wealth and luxury, Francis spent much of his youth seeking pleasure and enjoying popularity. But he turned his back on everything to embrace God, live a life of poverty, and serve lepers and the lowly. At first he was rejected by family and friends as a kook or a fanatic. But the compelling example of his life, combined with his persuasive preaching, soon brought him followers—first a handful, then thousands.

Today, Francis is revered as the most popular of saints. His feast day in October, often celebrated by the blessing of animals, is honored all over the world. Thousands of churches bear his name. But in the early thirteenth century, Francis's fervent faith provided a dramatic contrast with the moribund medieval Christianity.

The church of the Middle Ages was a big, wealthy, bureaucratically entrenched and politically influential institution whose leaders seemed more like self-centered, power-hungry civil authorities than selfless servants of God and humanity. Even many monasteries, which had been created as refuges for piety, became islands of wealth and worldliness.

But Francis was empowered and inflamed with a burning love for God. Simply and profoundly, he took the words of Jesus to his heart, understood what they meant in his mind, and sought out ways he could practice them in his life. He did all of this in a wild and carefree way, not stopping to calculate how it might hurt his career or cramp his lifestyle.

The people of Assisi, including Francis's churchgoing parents, were aghast. Why had this merchant's son traded his fashionable clothes for the rags of a beggar? Why was this playboy hanging out with lepers? Had he lost his mind?

The infectious, passionate, no-holds-barred faith of Francis soon ignited a movement of men and women who fanned out throughout Europe and the rest of the world. Today, there are more than one hundred thousand Franciscans in North America, as well as more than a million others worldwide. These followers of Francis make up the largest order in the Catholic Church.

Down through the ages, many people have sought to follow Francis's example in their lives, including King Louis IX of France, the poet Dante, the artist Michelangelo, the musician Arlo Guthrie, the scientist Michael Faraday, the philosopher Roger Bacon, and numerous theologians. Among that multitude I gratefully count myself and the small group of followers who live with me at the Little Portion, a community of men, women, and children nestled in the Ozark Mountains of Arkansas.

I believe Francis remains a powerful and reliable spiritual guide for our own troubled times.

His teaching is true, and his holiness should arouse our admiration.—St. Bonaventure

The worldwide influence of Francis can be measured by how many rivers, mountains, and cities, such as San Francisco, bear his name. He has also had a powerful influence on the world's great thinkers, inspiring thousands of books and studies, numerous motion pictures and documentaries, and dozens of musical compositions. Francis has been hailed by historians, praised by religious leaders, quoted by presidents, embraced by members of the 1960s youth counterculture, and even honored by Communist leaders as "the liberator of the medieval proletariat."

Though small of stature and plain in appearance, Francis has inspired hundreds of artistic masterpieces, including a renowned painting by Rembrandt. A devout Protestant who cared little for Catholicism, Rembrandt had a strong distaste for popery and the church's practice of canonizing saints. But he lovingly painted Francis, kneeling in front of an open Bible and clutching a crucifix to his chest, thus showing how this humble believer speaks to all who follow Christ, regardless of denominational affiliation.

Once a year, millions of people around the world remember the birth of Jesus with Nativity scenes. In doing so, they pay tribute to Francis, the worldly saint who created the first crèche in an effort to communicate the powerful paradox of God's son being born amid the hay and dung of a primitive stable.

Francis's love for all of creation, his sermons to the birds of the air and the flowers of the fields, and his rapturous communion with the cosmos have led to his enshrinement in millions of bird feeders and garden statues. And in 1980 he was named patron saint of ecology by the Catholic Church.

He strove to bend his own will to the will of God.
—THOMAS OF CELANO

These are just some of the highlights of the life of Francis, which is covered in more detail in chapter 14. I sympathize with the frustrated Franciscan biographer who wrote, "Human pens are really overpowered by the greatness of his wonderful life." Here are just a few thoughts about why Francis is such a universally popular figure and why I believe he is a trustworthy and reliable spiritual guide for us today.

▧ He Practiced What He Preached

At a time like ours, when wrapping oneself in the rhetoric of godliness is a sure way to win votes, gain respect, or sell books and records, Francis is a startling example of someone who lived his faith more than he talked about it. In his many private moments, as well as in his relationships with his followers and his public ministry, Francis pointed a probing finger at himself and his own weaknesses and shortcomings instead of busying himself with the failings of others.

By the example of his simple and radically committed life, Francis revealed a sometimes mysterious Christ to a world that could not, or often would not, see him. Even now, centuries after his death, that living example speaks more eloquently than a mountain of books, more forcefully than a lifetime of sermons.

▦ He Was Real

Books about the lives of some saints read like religious fairy tales, devoid of all dramatic tension or suspense. But because he came to God from a life of worldly success and carefree disbelief, Francis is the opposite of an otherworldly stained-glass saint.

A successful businessman who was a regular participant in Assisi's rowdy nightlife, Francis was on his way to triumphs in war when he was laid low by a debilitating illness and visited by a series of mystical visions. Over a period of years, he struggled to find God and understand the purpose of his life through an unsteady progress of stops and starts.

In some ways, the conversion of Francis is similar to that of Buddha, who experienced enlightenment after years spent in spiritual darkness. Saintly without being sanctimonious, Francis knew sin firsthand, not merely as an abstract theological dogma. And unlike other saints, whose lives are often obscured by halos and hagiography, Francis had his feet firmly planted on the ground, while his heart soared to heaven.

▦ He Was Radical

For many people, being "Christian" is roughly equivalent in time and emotional commitment to being a member of a neighborhood bridge club, having a regular seat at the local Elks lodge, or getting the family car serviced every three thousand miles. Unfortunately, this type of Christianity is often viewed as just another civic affiliation, acquired habit, or social ritual.

Not for Francis. In him, the spark of divine love ignited a bonfire that burned away all his indifference and sparked a radical, uncompromising faith. His was no Christianity Lite. He worshiped at the altar of no watered-down deity.

Francis's minute-by-minute desire was to follow God ever closer, as he wrote in this prayer to members of his movement: "Almighty, eternal, just and merciful God, grant us in our misery that we may do for your sake alone what we know you want us to do, and always want what pleases you; so that, cleansed and enlightened interiorly and fired with the ardor of the Holy Spirit, we may be able to follow in the footsteps of your Son, our Lord Jesus Christ, and so make our way to you."

▦ He Was Loving

Francis was overcome by divine love and wanted to be closer to God. Likewise, people who came into contact with Francis could sense his love for them, and were drawn closer to his embracing warmth, his compassionate concern, and his willingness to spend himself in serving their needs. His was no stern judgmentalism, remote transcendentalism, or icy intellectualism.

Perhaps because he had so often seen weakness and folly in himself, Francis was extremely tolerant of it in others. Or perhaps because he was so keenly aware of the extreme sufferings of Christ in his efforts to redeem the world, Francis felt moved to share and soothe the suffering of others. Although he was hard on himself and followed a life of extreme asceticism and self-imposed poverty, Francis was gentle with everyone else.

When clashes over religion and deeply held values divide people around our world, we can learn much from Francis, a model of respect and civility. Born during the Crusades, the centuries-long mother of all holy wars, Francis sought ways to be loving toward Muslims at a time when much of Christendom sought only to massacre them.

▨ He Was Passionate

For Francis, God was not a dry theological concept, and the Christian life was not a collection of dusty religious rules and rituals. Instead, his faith was that of a man who passionately and desperately loved God. Like any true lover, he did crazy things which could only be explained by that love; his enthusiastic behavior was often embarrassing both to himself and his followers.

The biographies of Francis are full of numerous

accounts of his outrageous behavior. For example, one night, the citizens of Assisi were awoken from their sleep by a noisy Francis. But this wasn't the rowdy Francis of old, who had promenaded through the city's streets late at night, singing and carousing with his friends. Rather, this night a solitary Francis was struck by the majestic beauty of the moon hanging in a dark, starlit sky. Overcome by the sheer beauty of the moment, and wanting to share it with the world, he stole into the town's church, ascended its bell tower, and began furiously ringing the bells. "Lift up your eyes, my friends," he cried out to his curious and angry neighbors. "Lift up your eyes. Look at the moon!"

Describing Francis, St. Bonaventure wrote, "He seemed to be completely absorbed by the fire of divine love like a glowing coal." And this warm glow was reflected in the way he related to others, treated animals, and respected nature. His reverence for God made him passionate about everything God had made.

▓ He Gives Us Hope

There's a scene in *Brother Sun, Sister Moon*, Franco Zeffirelli's film about Francis, that captures for me the essence of this saint. The setting is one of stark contrasts: Francis and a handful of his shabbily dressed followers are standing amid the pomp and glory of the Vatican court. Francis, who has come to ask the pope for his blessing, speaks joyfully about the beauty of the natural world and the incomparable gift of God's loving grace.

Struck by Francis's guileless simplicity, the pope says, "My dearest son, in our obsession with Original Sin, we too often forget—original innocence."

Francis's emphasis on innocence, hope, and the positive possibilities of faith in God gives me encouragement that underneath all the barnacles and cultural accretions that burden Christianity and obscure it from view there is a pure, powerful heartbeat of love that draws us closer to God, our creator and redeemer.

> *St. Francis walked the world like the Pardon of God.*—G. K. CHESTERTON

The life of Francis still confounds religious stereotypes, and it still presents to open minds and hearts an unprecedented view of what the Christian life is all about, as I can personally attest.

In 1968, a period of social turmoil and heightened spiritual searching was under way. I was a fifteen-year-old country rock star, traveling across America with my brother Terry in our band, Mason Proffit, which performed at packed concerts with artists like the Grateful Dead, Jefferson Airplane, and Janis Joplin. In six popular albums, our band preached a message of idealism and social concern centered around a few key issues, such as pacifism, racial tolerance, and environmentalism.

I was thrilled to be a part of a burgeoning youth movement that demanded answers to hard questions and sought to reinvent society from the bottom up. But certain inconsistencies in the movement startled and troubled me. Protesters arguing for peace were not opposed to using violence if it suited their needs. People searching for mystical revelation experimented with mind-transforming drugs, but then became so clouded and myopic that they lost all passion for spiritual pursuits, or any concerns beyond their own chemically souped-up egos.

My own hunger for spiritual answers became ravenous. Convinced that Christianity was part of the problem rather than part of the solution, I dug deeply into other spiritual paths, studying Buddhism, Hinduism, and especially Native American religions. Then the tables were turned on me as the truth I was so desperately searching for sought me out.

I was alone in a room in a Holiday Inn during the band's 1971 tour. I'm not sure what city I was in, but I vividly remember what happened there. My room filled with a brilliant light, and in the midst of the light was Jesus, dressed in white robes and with his arms stretched out toward me in a gesture of both gentleness and strength.

At the time, America was experiencing a religious revival called the Jesus movement, as millions of long-haired ex-hippies came to Christ. I began studying with some of these exuberant new converts and, before I knew it, I became a fuming fundamentalist, a walking, talking Jesus freak who would quote the Bible or dispense judgment at the drop of a hat. If you had a problem, I had a Bible verse for you. I was angry, I was arrogant, and I was horrible to be around, all in the name of Jesus.

I knew something was wrong and wrestled with soul-searching questions. Hadn't I done everything my Christian friends had asked me to do? Hadn't I become everything they had told me to become? But I knew the Christianity I was living out and the Christianity I saw around me were nothing like what I read about in the Gospels.

Then an evangelical friend gave me a copy of a book about Francis by Franciscan priest Murray Bodo. I read the book and I wept. I realized how far from genuine Christianity I had fallen, even though the desire of my heart was to follow Christ. As I read, I realized that Francis had done it: He had lived a balanced and beautiful Christian life.

As I continued reading about this amazing saint, I realized he was the genuine article. He had lived a life of poverty when all I was seeing were typical, upper-middle-class American Christians trying to balance their love for God with their love for money. He lived a life of mystical connection to God when all I saw was a cold and rationalistic form of Christianity that was all head and no heart. He lived a life of gentleness when all I saw was an arrogant, aggressive, my-way-or-the-highway Christianity. He lived a life of joy and radical commitment, when all I saw was an antiseptic, pedantic, down-the-middle-of-the-road meat-and-potatoes kind of Christianity that killed the spirit and squashed the joy.

In 1978, after a painful divorce, I began a sincere effort to follow in the footsteps of Francis, retreating to a hand-built hermitage in the Indiana woods where

I focused all of my being on knowing and following the will of God. In 1983, I helped found an exciting, new Franciscan community in the Ozark Mountains. Today, I and millions of others remain committed to the ideal that Francis's life is a pattern for our lives.

When someone asks me what it is about Francis that attracts me, I want to respond by painting a picture. There's a distinct look and feel to Francis. His life conjures up images of the tattered hem of Jesus' garment on a dusty Galilean road. His rugged and radical life feels like the rough wood of a cross. His life smells like the earth of a medieval Italian roadway, or the fragrance of a forest full of beautiful pines, tall poplars, rugged olive trees, and fruit-laden grapevines.

At a time when millions of people are hungering for spirituality but are turned off by many traditional churches, the life of Francis demonstrates that there *is* something to fill the God-shaped vacuum in our lives. That there *is* an answer to our soul's every longing. That the dream of inner and outer peace isn't an illusion. And that the potential person that God created us to be needn't remain lost and unrealized.

I also believe this: Even though some religious institutions may often look more like secular corporations than godly communities, Francis shows us that there's always room in churches for people guided by a radical spiritual commitment.

[Saints are] fellow human beings, at once tempted and tried, hugely given over to spiritual passions, insistently intent on realizing them in word, in deed, no matter what the personal consequences.

—ROBERT COLES

Once someone is officially named a saint, there's a danger that veneration will replace imitation, that people will stop at honoring and respecting the person instead of following his or her example and applying those lessons to daily life.

Francis was a godly person, and it thrills me that you have enough interest in him to read this book. I pray that your effort will be repaid with interest. But the point of studying the life of Francis—or any other saint—doesn't end with hanging his picture on the wall, buying a Francis bird feeder for your garden, and going on with your life untouched.

My goal, and the purpose of this book, is to help you find ways to learn from his life and apply these lessons to the complex and often messy job of living each day in a spiritually genuine way. And that's why this book includes questions to challenge you, suggested activities you can try, and simple prayers to help guide you on your spiritual journey.

In the following pages are chapters exploring key Franciscan ideals like simplicity, creativity, and solitude. You'll also find excerpts from Francis's writings (including poems, prayers, letters, and the various rules he wrote for his followers), passages from many early biographies, and quotations from a variety of saints and sages, old and new. I've selected these excerpts because they show the universal appeal of Francis's life and teaching, and demonstrate how his spirituality speaks to our common yearning for deep joy and fulfillment. My hope is that this book will be a useful guide to helping you live your own life, and my prayer is that while you're reading, you'll open your mind to new ways of living and open your heart to God.

2
Simplicity

Because they had nothing, they feared in no way to lose anything.

—THOMAS OF CELANO

JUST OUTSIDE THE INDIANA FARMHOUSE WHERE I lived as a young man stood several large mulberry trees that seemed like they were a part of the house, or even members of our family.

One day these beloved trees endured a three-hour attack by a uniformed professional crew wielding chain saws and hydraulic ladders. Quickly and efficiently the crew sawed, trimmed, and pruned the trees, reducing a large and leafy mass to a skeleton of a few stark, naked limbs hanging from lonely trunks surrounded by mounds of sawdust and leaves.

I felt certain the trees would never recover from the assault. But to my surprise, the following spring the trees grew larger and fuller than ever before, bursting forth in an extravagant display of flowers, leaves, and mulberries. Instead of killing off my beloved trees, the process of pruning helped them blossom into their fullest productivity.

What's good for mulberry trees is good for us, too, and the virtue of simplicity is a time-tested tool that we can use to prune our lives. Voluntarily submitting our lives to an ongoing pruning process removes our irregularities, trims our unproductive growth, and prepares us for a future of fruitfulness and productivity.

In the next few pages, we'll look at simplicity, a spiritual practice that has been at the center of the monastic way of life for centuries. I believe that if you are willing to practice simplicity, a sometimes challenging way of life that is both immensely practical and deeply spiritual, you can greatly enrich your life.

> *The love of money is a root of all kinds of evil.*
>
> —St. Paul

It seems that if ever there was a time when the virtue of simplicity was desperately needed, it's in our own fast-paced, consumer-oriented, information-overloaded era. But Francis had good reasons for believing his own day needed a big dose of simple living.

Living during a time when money was rapidly replacing barter as the primary medium of exchange, Francis saw huge socioeconomic barriers between the haves and the have-nots. The carnality of his age seemed to overwhelm everything, including the church, which was one of the most powerful international banking institutions of the Middle Ages. "All, from the highest to the lowest, allow themselves to be led by avarice," wrote Pope Innocent III, protesting his age's rising tide of greed. He wasn't complaining about small-scale capitalists like Francis's father; instead, he was condemning the greed of the clergy!

Francis spent the first twenty-four years of his life in luxury and indulgence. But he spent the next twenty-one years in austere, self-imposed poverty, the result of his life-changing encounter with the living Christ and his no-holds-barred commitment to follow the example of Jesus, whose earthly life was a model of simple living, from his birth in a dingy stable to his Crucifixion on a common criminal's cross.

As Francis reflected on the life and words of Jesus, he was confronted time and time again with Christ's simple lifestyle, his warnings about the dangers of money, and his commandments to his followers to sell all they owned and give the profits to the poor.

In Francis's day as in our own, this radical Jesus wasn't the subject of many Sunday sermons. But as he studied the teachings of Jesus, Francis was inspired by the many lessons on simplicity, including this one, from the Sermon on the Mount:

> Do not worry about your life, what you will eat or drink; or about your body, what you will wear. Is not life more important than food, and the body more important than clothes? Look at the birds of the air; they do not sow or reap or store away in barns, and yet your heavenly Father feeds them. . . . And why do you worry about clothes? See how the lilies of the field grow. They do not labor or spin. Yet I tell you that not even Solomon in all his splendor was dressed like one of these. If that is how God clothes the grass of

the field, which is here today and tomorrow is thrown into the fire, will he not much more clothe you, O you of little faith?

Francis and his followers didn't view simplicity as a specialized discipline for monks or other unusual individuals seeking advanced degrees in enlightenment. Instead, they saw it as the garden from which all other spiritual virtues grow, and as a prerequisite to our being both fully human and fully spiritual.

Like the branches of an unpruned tree, our attachment to possessions and wealth often chokes our lives, enslaves our souls, and hinders both human community and union with God. Francis prescribed simplicity as an antidote to our often unquenchable yearning for more and ever more.

If we had any possessions we should be forced to have arms to protect them, since possessions are a cause of disputes and strife, and in many ways we should be hindered from loving God and our neighbor. Therefore, in this life, we wish to have no temporal possessions.—FRANCIS

As long as there have been cities, civilizations, or technology, sensitive souls have sounded an alarm about the corrosive consequences of chaos and complexity.

In 1845, writer and naturalist Henry David Thoreau turned his back on the hustle and bustle of Concord, Massachusetts, built a simple cabin in the woods near Walden Pond, and spent two years, two months, and two days there, concentrating only on what he called "the essential facts of life." "Our life is frittered away by detail," he wrote in his classic work, *Walden*. "Simplify, simplify."

More than a century later, E. F. Schumacher's *Small Is Beautiful*, an eloquent manifesto about the threat of technology and economic growth run rampant, helped inspire a growing concern for simpler ways of living. His philosophy has found expression in a variety of movements emphasizing conservation, ecology, sustainable lifestyles, natural foods, and social and economic justice.

While these movements have been helpful for some, they have done little for millions who are regularly run ragged by too much tension, too many choices, and too little peace in a life that is spinning wildly out of control. According to one noted psychologist, twenty to thirty million Americans suffer from anxiety symptoms every year, while sales of antidepressant drugs like Prozac are booming.

Clearly, something is out of balance when millions of people are wracked by stress and medicated against despair. Not that life is a picnic. Hardly. Daily living can be full of challenge and pain. But many people unnecessarily complicate their lives, and suffer from a nagging unhappiness that in some ways results directly from their own misguided search for peace and happiness.

Less is more.—ROBERT BROWNING

Thankfully, a solution for this dilemma can be found in the centuries-old monastic tradition. Most monasteries practice some form of communal ownership of goods, like the first Christian believers, who according to the book of Acts, "were together and had all things in common."

From the earliest days of the Franciscan movement, followers of Francis have practiced a second form of simplicity called the "mendicant" or "open-handed" approach. This approach is inspired by the way in which Jesus sent his disciples out into the world: They were not to take with them gold, silver, copper, bags, changes of clothes, sandals, or even a walking staff.

Admittedly, both approaches may seem somewhat extreme, and both are probably impractical and unappealing for the vast majority of people. But Francis teaches us about yet another way to practice simplicity.

> *I tell you the truth, unless you change and become like little children, you will never enter the kingdom of heaven.*—JESUS

Francis, who was described by one biographer as a "very rich poor man," lived the second half of his life with very few possessions: "From the first moment of his religious life until his death, his sole wealth consisted in a habit, a cord, and a pair of trousers, and he was content with that."

Still, those who cared for Francis continually gave him cloaks and coats to protect him from the cold weather. But it was a fruitless effort. As soon as the saint saw someone else who was also in need, he would remove the donated clothing and give it away.

Handing a cloak to a beggar one day, Francis said, "We only got it on loan until we found someone in greater need of it." When his friars complained, Francis responded, "God the great Almsgiver will regard it as a theft on my part, if I do not give what I have to someone who needs it."

Through such lessons the deeper truths of Francis's message of simplicity become clear: Living your life engrossed in the cares and chaos of the world is not only bad for you, it's bad for others as well.

Although North Americans make up only a small percentage of the world's population, they consume a large amount of the world's limited resources. Ours is a world in which a few possess much, while many don't have enough to meet even their most basic needs. This chasm of disparity calls out for a compassionate response, and part of that response can be found in simple living.

Live simply so that others may simply live.—GANDHI

You don't need to be an itinerant or a monk to follow God's call to simplicity. Francis describes a third, more mainstream model: practicing equality in a world of savage disparity. Like other Franciscan approaches, this one also has a basis in the Bible. Paul, in his second letter to the Christians at Corinth, encouraged those believers to consider the welfare of others: "as a matter of equality your surplus at the present time should supply [others'] needs, so that their surplus may also supply your needs, that there may be equality."

This equality-based model for simple living is both a matter of urgent practicality and a potent symbol of spiritual intent. The effort to simplify and consume less is a real way to decrease our emphasis on self-gratification and increase our ability to share with others. Simplifying our lives and denying some of our incessant cravings is also a powerful way to symbolically enter into the suffering of others around the world.

> *Manifest plainness, embrace simplicity, reduce selfishness, have few desires.*—LAO-TZU

When the professional pruners came to do battle with our family's mulberry trees, they didn't remove all the limbs, cut through the trunks, or damage the roots. Instead of harming the parts of the trees that were essential for health and growth, they focused their efforts on out-of-control limbs and branches. Likewise, we don't need to plunge into abject poverty when we hear the call to simplify our lives.

But there is one important step we can take that helps us begin the process of living more simply. That step involves distinguishing between our wants and our needs.

It's difficult for North Americans who have grown up on a steady diet of capitalism, consumer culture, and advertising to distinguish between things they really need and things they merely want. In fact, one of the primary purposes of advertising is to blur this important distinction, magnetically attracting us to a nearby shopping mall where we buy bags of things that advertisers promise will make us happy and make our lives complete.

How do we sort through the confusion? Here's a

simple formula for distinguishing between our wants and our needs:

✤ Food is a need. But a medium-rare T-bone steak smothered in onions is a want.
✤ Clothing is a need. But a designer suit with matching shoes is a want.
✤ Housing is a need. But a split-level ranch house with a semiattached garage, walk-in closets, and three bathrooms is a want.

Not all wants are bad or destructive. For example, I'm a musician. I have a nice guitar and a better-than-average stereo. And I devote much of my time and energy to composing and performing music, even though I realize that music is a want, not a need. But I still consider music and other creative arts as essential ingredients of a full and well-rounded life. Unlike trees, which can survive on a steady diet of sun and rain, people need intangibles like beauty and joy to thrive.

Francis is not some fun-impaired fanatic who wants to whack our fingers with a ruler every time we grasp anything pleasurable. Not all wants are bad. But a life consumed by fulfilling all our wants is a recipe for frustration and unhappiness. If we seek to practice simplicity, distinguishing between wants and needs will help us prune our lives and cut away the things that hinder our growth.

Francis and his followers were comforted exceedingly in the absence of all things that are of this world.
—Thomas of Celano

Daily life forces us to make hundreds of decisions, many of them seemingly unimportant. But if we consistently apply the ideal of simplicity to even the mundane choices in our lives, we can begin living simply in the midst of a complex and often confusing culture.

By practicing simplicity and pruning the tangled branches of our lives, we will be doing two things at once. First, we will cut back the areas of our lives that have grown wildly out of control and threaten to kill us or drive us crazy. And second, we will channel our future growth toward a simpler approach to living that will leave us less subject to future headaches and heartaches.

Food, clothing, and shelter are three basic human needs, but in many people's lives, these needs are overgrown and uncontrolled. Here's a look at how we can begin applying the rich and incredibly practical Franciscan tradition of simplicity to these three areas.

> *Francis' greatest concern was to be free from everything of this world, lest the serenity of his mind be disturbed even for an hour by the taint of anything that was mere dust.*—THOMAS OF CELANO

What's wrong with this picture? North Americans spend billions on lavish eating, on diets that contain too many harmful substances and too little of the necessary proteins and nutrients. Plus, we spend billions more on dieting pills, potions, and programs in an effort to escape the natural consequences of our consumption. In fact, we spend more on diet aids than the people of many nations spend on food.

Balance and moderation in eating have been part of the Judeo-Christian tradition for millennia, as the book of Sirach, part of the Jewish wisdom literature, makes clear:

> Moderate eating ensures sound slumber
> and a clear mind next day on rising . . .
> In whatever you do, be moderate,
> and no sickness will befall you.

Francis stressed moderation in eating, too. And here's how we at the Little Portion community try to practice moderation and simplicity in our diets.

For one thing, we take advantage of our rural location to grow our own vegetables and raise our own chickens and goats, which provide us with fresh eggs, meat, and milk. This enables us to produce healthy and affordable food while avoiding the hazards of an agribusiness-dominated food industry that depends on high-tech equipment and large doses of chemical fertilizers, herbicides, and pesticides, which harm the food supply and pollute our fragile environment.

While it may be impossible for you to begin a mini-farm in your front yard, you may be able to grow small amounts of lettuce, tomatoes, or strawberries in a garden. And if you can afford it, your body will appreciate naturally grown fruits and vegetables.

A second thing we do at Little Portion is promote vegetable protein. We derive the majority of the protein in our diets from beans, rice, and other protein-rich foods, which are easy to prepare and inexpensive.

Beyond nutrition and cost issues, we believe there are

powerful ethical reasons to cut down the amount of meat in our diets. For one thing, producing meat requires much more land, water, and other natural resources than does growing vegetables and grains. Furthermore, large meat-producing facilities often subject animals to horrible conditions. Francis stressed that animals are God's creatures and deserve ethical treatment. And even though he wasn't a vegetarian, I'd bet a bag of beans that he would become one if he saw the conditions animals endure at many agribusiness complexes today.

A third part of our effort to simplify our eating consists of occasionally not eating! Of course, monks and mystics over the centuries have called this fasting. Jesus did it regularly, particularly when he was approaching a crucial period in his ministry. Francis did it often, and frequently he was carried away into experiences of serene spiritual euphoria. Fasting is something members of our community do twice a week, thus reaping a windfall of physical and spiritual benefits.

We find that fasting on bread and water is a wonderful discipline which teaches us the difference between wants and needs while allowing us to empathize with the hunger of the poor. If done with proper care, fasting can be a powerful practice that cleanses the body of impurities, enhances the power of the mind, sensitizes us to the needs of the spirit, breaks our addictions to unhealthy eating habits, and makes a significant symbolic statement about the desire to stand against the excesses of consumer culture.

All the poor friars must wear poor clothes and they can patch them with pieces of sackcloth and other material, with God's blessing.—RULE OF ST. FRANCIS

Monks don't spend hours standing in front of their closets every morning wondering about what clothes they're going to put on. For me, the choices are simple: this basic brown habit, or that basic brown habit.

My garment is a simple one in a complex, showy world that places inordinate emphasis on style, fashion, and in-your-face sexuality. And my habit is widely accepted, whether I'm performing before thousands, walking through a dusty Third World village, or meeting with religious and social leaders.

Contrast the Franciscans' simple wardrobe with the nearly $100 billion a year North Americans spend on clothing, grooming, and fashion. Surprisingly, for all that money we spend, most of us get clothes that are uncomfortable, uncomplimentary, unhealthy, and almost instantly out-of-date.

Maybe you aren't ready to adopt the monk's simple habit, but there are still many ways you can prune your wardrobe and begin the process of moving from wants to needs, and from fashion slavery to simple living.

Begin by creating a small but versatile wardrobe. Instead of having pants or dresses and complete sets of matching accessories in every color of the rainbow (plus hundreds of new man-made hues), start with basic blacks, browns, beiges, or blues. Add variety by carefully choosing a few colorful shirts or tops that can be varied easily. Focus on a few basic outfits you can modify with ease instead of having a closet full of expensive and seldom-worn clothes.

If you're like most people, chances are your closets currently contain clothes that you hardly ever wear. Why not pare down your holdings and share your wardrobe wealth with a homeless shelter or other agency in your town that can make your surplus clothing available free or at low cost to people who truly need it.

And be on guard against shopping sprees. Decide what you need before getting near a shopping mall. And try to resist being overly influenced by persuasive advertising or perceived social pressure.

One goes more quickly to heaven from a hut than from a palace.—FRANCIS

The opera *Clari, or, the Maid of Milan*, includes the classic line, "Be it ever so humble, there's no place like home." But in Francis's day, as in our own, many homes were far from humble. Today, many people live in expensive, roomy houses that are a hassle to keep clean and a challenge to afford. Instead of living close to the earth, we build monuments to our egos and our needs for social acceptance.

If you have a nice home, there's no need to feel guilty. But consider making your house a place where others can feel loved and welcomed by practicing hospitality and feeding, housing, and entertaining people who have nowhere else to go. As for the future, maybe you can keep the house you've got instead of constantly trading up into more impressive and expensive models. Plus, some people find peace and security in cohousing or semicommunal arrangements, where a cluster of private homes share common social and recreational areas.

▦ Putting Simplicity into Practice

Is your life so hectic that you feel anxious, out of control, or depressed? Are you so busy working to make money to buy time-saving devices that you don't have any time to use them? Do you spend more time taking care of your possessions than you do enjoying your relationships with others and God?

If so, sit down for a few minutes and reflect on the following questions:

1. Do I have some possessions that complicate my life but don't really bring me any enjoyment?
2. What are some things that do bring me enjoyment but may not be worth the cost in time, money, and concern?
3. Do I buy things that I don't need, won't use, or can't afford?
4. What do I really need, and what do I merely want?
5. Am I consuming more than my fair share of the world's limited resources? What am I doing to help those who are less fortunate than myself? Is there some of my surplus that could benefit others with less?

Pray about simplifying your life. Here's a basic prayer you can use as a model: "God, give me new eyes to see my life as you see it. And give me a new heart to sense the difference between my wants and my needs. Give me compassion for the suffering of the world, and a willingness to help those who are hurting. Amen."

When you have more time, examine the following three areas of your life in greater detail.

✦ Food

Walk around your kitchen, look in your cupboards and nose around your refrigerator. Then ask yourself these questions:

1. Do I regularly buy things that I don't eat, waste, or throw away?
2. How many varieties of cereal, soup, spice, or mustard do I really need?
3. Is my diet balanced and healthy? Do I eat enough fruits and vegetables? Am I consuming too much fat and too many calories, while starving myself of protein and nutrients?
4. Are there ways I can spend less to get more nutrition?

✦ Clothing

Look in your closets and drawers. Count the number of pants (or dresses) you have. Now count shirts, sweaters, and shoes. Ask the following questions:

1. When was the last time you wore some of the items you possess? When do you plan to wear them again? Could they better benefit someone else?
2. What colors accentuate the color of your hair, eyes, and complexion? Can you base a wardrobe around these colors?
3. How can you build a basic wardrobe that can be adapted easily to a multitude of social and professional settings instead of having complete wardrobes for every moment of your life?

✚ *Shelter*

Walk in and around your house or apartment and take the following inventory:

1. How much space do I and other family members really need? Will we need more or less space in the future?
2. Do I look at my house as a shelter, or is it a status symbol designed to impress neighbors and friends?
3. Are there possessions in our house that we don't use and only cramp our living space? Can we get rid of these, and avoid buying more unnecessary stuff?

'Tis the gift to be simple
'Tis the gift to be free
'Tis the gift to come down where we ought to be.
—TRADITIONAL SHAKER HYMN

Francis had much more to say about the dangers of money than about a host of other subjects. Knowing that our attitude toward material things can be an important part of our spiritual growth and development, Francis denounced money as "flies," commanded his followers to discard coins in a pile of animal dung, and sought every opportunity to deny himself the pleasures of wealth and comfort.

But Francis never claimed his way of life was for everyone. And in another example of the balance he sought between extremes, he told his followers not to criticize or condemn people who were wealthy and had nice things: "I admonish and exhort them not to despise or judge men whom they see clothed in fine and showy garments, using dainty meats and drinks, but rather let each one judge and despise himself."

As you can see, the practice of simplicity isn't necessarily simple or easy. Like the pruning of a tree, the practice of simplicity requires that things be cut away, sometimes with pain. But in the long run, this is a practice that enables us to live life with more joy, peace, and happiness.

Many of us are so busy that we accomplish little of any real value. We are so consumed by our many possessions that we never experience what it means to have much. Many of us spend less time with our families, or with God, than did primitive hunter-gatherers who lived lives of subsistence and daily survival.

Simplicity is God's grand antidote to a culture of

money and madness. And properly understood and lived out, simplicity is God's pruning shear, which cuts back the tangled branches of our lives, enabling us to begin living freely, sharing generously, and loving deeply.

3

Joy

The safest remedy against the thousand snares and wiles of the enemy is spiritual joy.—FRANCIS

THE PEOPLE OF GRECCIO PROBABLY WONDERED what Francis was doing in the stable outside of their town on Christmas eve in the year 1223. But to the stable they went, even though it was bitterly cold, because they were intrigued to see what Francis, a popular but unpredictable preacher and holy man, was up to now.

When they first saw what he had done, they didn't know how to take it all in. For there in a manger was a tiny baby, wrapped snugly in strips of cloth and warmed by the hot, steamy breath of a half dozen cows and sheep. But soon, their confusion gave way to joy, as they began to share Francis's innocent delight.

There in that humble barn in a backwoods Italian town, the joy of Christmas became palpable through the Nativity scene, a lifelike reenactment of the birth of Jesus that tells volumes more about the true meaning of

Christmas than do our glitzy celebrations and over-crowded shopping malls.

For Francis, it wasn't enough to simply acknowledge the birth of Jesus with the reading of a few passages of Scripture and the singing of a few songs. He wanted to dive into the event, and experience it with all his senses.

Somehow, not everyone shares the intuitive joy of Francis. One Christmas, one of the friars of his order came to Francis with a more mundane concern. Christmas Day was to come on a Friday, meaning that a traditional feast day fell on a day usually reserved for fasting from meat. What should we do, asked the brother, feast or fast?

Francis's response was sure and swift: "You sin, brother, calling the day on which the Child was born to us a day of fast. It is my wish that even the walls should eat meat on such a day."

> *The universe is not a random assortment of atoms and fiery globes spinning and whirling in empty space to their destruction. Rather it is a symphony of rhythm and harmony that expresses the pleasure of its Creator. Divine joy was and is the primal reason for its existence. And, one might add, for ours also.*
>
> —SHERWOOD WIRT

Reading about the life of Francis is like stepping onto some kind of religious roller coaster. His passionate and sometimes impulsive emotional life was full of lofty peaks as well as deep, dark valleys. But one thing's for sure: It wasn't bland.

Thomas of Celano, a follower of Francis and one of his earliest biographers, frequently described the simple saint's religious reveries: "Sometimes this most holy man was out of his mind for God in a wonderful manner." Francis could be inspired to heights of inexpressible joy by the sight of a butterfly or the scent of a flower. One biographer tells how Francis was overcome by the gentle music of a lute: "The holy father enjoyed so much the sweetness in that melodious song that he thought he had been transported to another world."

Of course, he could also experience great sorrow, brought about by the slightest recollection of the sorrows of his savior. Often, he experienced giddy joy and jarring grief simultaneously. He firmly believed that God, who created us with a vibrant set of emotions, wanted us to let those emotions be a part of how we experience life.

Occasionally, his fellow friars unintentionally stumbled upon Francis when he sought to express his overflowing joy: "Sometimes Francis would act in the following way. When the sweetest melody of spirit would bubble up in him, he would give exterior expression to it in French, and the breath of the divine whisper which his ear perceived in secret would burst forth in French in a song of joy.

"At times, as we saw with our own eyes, he would pick up a stick from the ground and putting it over his left arm, would draw across it, as across a violin, a little bow bent by means of a string; and going through the motions of playing, he would sing in French about his Lord. This whole ecstasy of joy would often end in tears."

Unfortunately, if Francis were alive today and brought his often messy bundle of emotions to a church near us, the ushers would promptly show him to the door. What a commentary on the death of the spirit in our day.

Happiness turns up more or less where you'd expect it to—a good marriage, a rewarding job, a pleasant vacation. Joy, on the other hand, is as notoriously unpredictable as the one who bequeaths it.

—FREDERICK BUECHNER

At this point, it's understandable if you're confused. After all, in the last chapter we talked about how Francis turned his back on earthly pleasures and worldly wealth to pursue a life of simplicity, poverty, and self-denial. But now, Francis has suddenly become a connoisseur of the arts and a man who drinks life to the dregs. Could this be the same man?

There's no contradiction here. Instead, Francis makes it perfectly clear that one of the main reasons he experienced deep joy was because he intentionally walked away from the things in life that steal our joy. Francis intuitively understood what the social critic Eric Hoffer meant when he said, "The search for happiness is one of the chief sources of unhappiness."

Like a life-term prisoner who wakes up one morning to find he has been pardoned and is free to leave his dank, dingy cell, Francis made a sudden break with his past and the cares of this world when he embraced his new life of service to God and humanity.

Francis got a helping hand from his father, who was growing tired of his son's newfound religiosity, particularly after Francis stole some of his merchandise to raise funds for rebuilding a church. In a final, futile effort to get his son to return to "normalcy" and the family business, his father hauled Francis before the Bishop of Assisi. But Francis was unbowed. He stripped himself naked, handed his clothes to his father, and walked away, adopting a beggar's simple tunic and a pilgrim's detachment toward the cares and snares of the world. As St. Bonaventure described it, "Now that he was free from the bonds of all earthly desires in his disregard for the world, Francis left the town; he was free and without a care in the world and he made the forest resound, as he sang God's praises."

This carefree, open-handed approach to life was also what characterized the beginnings of the Franciscan movement. People gave up all they owned to join Francis and his band of spiritual pilgrims, and in return they gained a level of joy that they could not contain.

Looking at the life of Francis, we can see that he knew the difference between a fleeting and often superficial happiness and a deep and abiding joy.

Receive poverty, want, sickness, and all miseries joyfully from the hand of God, and with equal joy receive consolation, refreshment, and all super-abundance.—MACARIUS THE ELDER·

Psalm 23 is one of the most beautiful and best-loved passages in all of Scripture. "The Lord is my shepherd, I shall not want," it begins. "Even though I walk through the valley of the shadow of death, I will fear no evil." For me, as for many others, that passage has provided great comfort, reminding me of God's loving presence in our lives, even in the midst of pain and sorrow.

I set that psalm to music after my father was struck down by a heart attack when I was twenty-five years old. I was shocked at how rapidly my father—a very self-assured person and respected businessman—was rendered nearly helpless in the prime of his life. During the course of a fatal bout with emphysema, caused in part by his habit of smoking five to six packs of cigarettes a day, he went from being strong and independent to being helpless and childlike.

But during the year he was hospitalized, two things happened that helped transform this situation from one of sadness into one of joy. For one thing, my father and I talked to each other in a way we had never talked before. There were so many wonderful exchanges during which we truly shared as father and son. But also, as my father's health continued to worsen, he began to think more about some of the deeper issues of life and death. Although he had been a churchgoer nearly all his life, he had never really had a relationship with God. Now, as his connection to this life began to loosen, he started to stretch out his hands to heaven in a desire to grasp the life that never ends.

After a while, my father decided he wanted to become a member of the Catholic Church. I remember we had a simple confirmation service in the hospital's little chapel. Joy and sadness were both present at that service. Everyone in the room was crying, because they knew my father was failing fast. But he was smiling. It wasn't long after that I sang Psalm 23 at his funeral.

All of us go through torment and suffering in our lives. There's no escape from that, even though self-help gurus tell us we can overcome anything with the right mental attitude, and a flood of marketing pitches makes it sound as if perfect peace comes with the purchase of the right shampoo or a new car. But Francis teaches us that what's really important is how we approach life's tragedies.

It would have been easy for me to become enraged at

God over my father's death. I could have demanded to know why he wasn't healing my father. I could have shook my fists at the heavens and cursed the fact that the world is shot through with illness and death. Instead, I looked for God's blessing in the midst of the tragedy. I thought of my father smiling. And I thought of God smiling as he welcomed my father to his side.

St. Bonaventure described Francis's gift for finding joy in the midst of tragedy: "Francis was at peace in his utter loyalty to God and he felt a heavenly joy in his heart which showed in his face, even in the midst of his tears."

For me, it's interesting to see that Francis composed music in the midst of death and tragedy, just as I had during my father's lengthy illness. One evening, as it became increasingly clear that Francis was approaching death himself, he offered a prayer of humble submission and acceptance to God. The next morning when he awoke, his imagination was ablaze with words and melodies, which he used to compose his "Canticle of the Sun," a sublime work of devotion to God and deep respect for creation that is still sung today.

If you want to experience profound joy, don't seek solace in skin-deep entertainments or protection in illusory safety from tragedy. Instead, seek a godly perspective that gives us eyes to distinguish the fleeting from the eternal, the shallow from the deep.

I've realized it's possible to fall into the trap of thinking a life of carefully limited emotions, a life without emotional highs and lows, is a life that pleases God most. But that often results in a tragic loss of vigor in individuals and in the family of God. Too many people spend too much time in the emotional land of bland. —BILL HYBELS

During your years in school, were you ever called into the principal's office? Or have you ever been summoned to a last-minute meeting with your boss? Depending on your grades or your job performance, such conferences may cause your stomach to tighten, your pulse to quicken, and your brow to furrow. Usually, such meetings are cause to be on your best behavior. And I would certainly think that most people would be serious and solemn if they were called to a meeting with the pope.

But not Francis. When a bishop helped Francis get an audience in Rome, there was a surprise in store for the bishop, the many cardinals, the entire papal court, and perhaps even the pope himself. For when Francis came before the pope, he didn't cower in fear or stand at attention. He danced.

Here's how Thomas of Celano tells it: "He spoke with such great fervor of spirit, that, not being able to contain himself for joy, when he spoke the words with his mouth, he moved his feet as though he were dancing."

What is it about some religious people—whether in Francis's day or our own—that makes them think God is a cosmic killjoy? That sanctity must lead straight to solemnity? That hymns must be funeral dirges? They certainly don't get such ideas from God, who rejoiced as he created the universe, or Jesus, whose first miracle was to turn water into wine at a wedding feast. Many people obviously don't understand what the anonymous medieval author of *The Cloud of Unknowing* meant when he talked about "the delight of the Lord's playfulness."

Many seem intent on remaking God in their own image—cautious and emotionally crippled—instead of embracing the fact that we are made in the image of God. Consider God, who can be gentle with a repentant sinner one minute and angry with a wayward world the next. Or consider Jesus, who wept openly at the death of a friend named Lazarus but who cast the moneychangers out of the Temple in a holy rage.

God didn't create us as heartless, soulless automatons. Instead, we were given feelings so we could experience life and everything in creation more deeply. Francis understood that.

Jesus said not: thou shalt not be troubled, thou shalt not be tempted, thou shalt not be distressed. But he said: thou shalt not be overcome.
—JULIAN OF NORWICH

Picture, for a moment, a flower. When it receives sufficient sunlight, it flourishes and grows. But if the light is cut off, it withers and dies. It's the same way with us. Joy is an essential ingredient to surviving and thriving in a world full of darkness and bad news.

Much has changed in the world since Francis died. For one thing, we're all surrounded by a worldwide network of satellites and media that can instantly transmit all the world's troubles to our homes. When there's a deadly earthquake in California or a devastating flood in Bangladesh, the images of death and despair flicker in our living rooms. But on the other hand, things haven't really changed all that much. Then as now, we all deal with dejection, an affliction that while not always fatal can, as Francis said, "generate an abiding rust in the heart."

Francis would have nothing to do with dejection. He condemned it as a poisonous ailment, and in the rule he wrote for his friars, he warned them against sliding into sadness: "Let the brothers beware lest they show themselves outwardly gloomy and sad hypocrites; but let them show themselves joyful in the Lord, cheerful and suitably gracious."

Francis cautioned the friars that Satan sought to exaggerate even the slightest dejections into full-fledged crises: "The Devil exults when he can extinguish or even impede the devotion and joy brought about by pure prayer or other good works in the heart of God's servant. If the Devil takes hold of a servant of God, and if the latter is not wise enough to eliminate this bond as soon as possible by confession, contrition, and satisfaction, it would be very easy for the Devil to take the slightest thing and turn it into an ever heavier burden."

These comments shouldn't be misunderstood. Francis isn't denying the reality of bad news, and he isn't telling us that we should try to convince ourselves that bad is good, that sadness is joy. Francis didn't run and hide from reality. He was fundamentally real. On the other hand, he did realize that dejection and depression can easily harden into a skeptical and cynical outlook on all of life. Such an outlook serves as a perverse kind of diabolical filter, blocking out the warm rays of God's healing love.

Here at Little Portion, one of the things we do is begin each day with a prayer of thanks to God. As we are in the act of waking from our sleep, the first thing out of our lips is the brief prayer: "Praise be to Jesus Christ, now and forever." It's a simple but profound way of opening a new day with a positive spirit rather than a complaining attitude. This simple tradition helps me embrace a new day, with all its potential and promise, instead of beginning my day by grumbling, as many do, about another lousy day of toil and stress.

> *I don't envy those who have never known any pain, physical or spiritual, because I strongly suspect that only those who have suffered great pain are able to know equally great joy.*—MADELEINE L'ENGLE

In addition to the run-of-the-mill problems of daily life, people who try to follow God sometimes endure additional persecution because of their faith.

In the Beatitudes, Jesus told his followers, "Blessed are you when people insult you, persecute you and falsely say all kinds of evil against you because of me. Rejoice and be glad because great is your reward in heaven, for in the same way they persecuted the prophets who were before you." And James the brother of Jesus, who headed the first Christian church at Jerusalem, began a letter with the following advice: "Consider it pure joy, my brothers, whenever you face trials of many kinds, because you know that the testing of your faith develops perseverance. Perseverance must finish its work so that you may be mature and complete, not lacking anything."

In his sincere desire to wholeheartedly apply the Gospel to his life, Francis embraced persecution as the emblem of God's love. From the beginning of his religious life (when townspeople jeered him, threw things at him, and called him a madman) to his later years (when he took risky journeys to visit Muslim rulers to talk to them about the Christian faith), Francis saw persecution as the smoke that accompanies the fire of a burning love for God. In his own life, he accepted persecution with joy. And in his instructions to members of his movement, he portrayed pain as part of the package that goes with a thoroughly spiritual lifestyle.

One bitterly cold winter day, Francis and a friar named Brother Leo were returning to St. Mary of the Angels monastery from a visit to a nearby town, when Francis launched into a minisermon on perfect joy. Perfect joy, he said, wasn't to be found in the success of his movement, in the ability to perform amazing miracles, in the possession of vast knowledge, or in the ability to preach with such beauty and effectiveness that all who heard would be converted.

After a few miles of such lecturing, Brother Leo became curious, so he asked, "Father, I beg you in God's name to tell me what perfect joy is."

"When we come to St. Mary of the Angels," Francis replied, "soaked by the rain and frozen by the cold, all soiled with mud and suffering from hunger, and we ring at the gate of the Place and the brother porter comes and says angrily: 'Who are you?' And we say: 'We are two of your brothers.' And he contradicts us, saying, 'You are not telling the truth. Rather you are two rascals who go around deceiving people and stealing what they give to the poor. Go away!' And he does not open for us, but makes us stand outside in the snow and rain, cold and hungry, until night falls—then if we endure all those insults and cruel rebuffs patiently, without being troubled and without complaining, and if we reflect humbly and charitably that the porter really knows us and that God makes him speak against us, oh, Brother Leo, write that perfect joy is there!"

Francis might seem like a fanatic here, if we didn't know the end of his sermon to Brother Leo: "Above all the graces and gifts of the Holy Spirit which Christ gives to his friends is that of conquering oneself and willingly enduring suffering, insults, humiliations, and hardships for the love of Christ."

Francis lived a life of such passionate devotion that he saw trials and tribulations as ways to test—and attest to—the depth of that devotion.

> *Restless are our hearts until they rest in thee.*
> —ST. AUGUSTINE

The Original Sin—which is called such because it was first, not because it's particularly creative—was the human pride of thinking we could outsmart God. Today, this unoriginal arrogance, this misplaced belief that we can control our lives and our destinies with no acknowledgment of any higher power or authority, is one of the chief barriers to joy.

Trying to control life and manufacture happiness leads to frustration, sadness, and anger. But Francis taught that joy comes from abandoning ourselves into the hands of God. Ironically, this submission to God doesn't result in a life that is defeatist, pessimistic, or separated from the rhythms of life. Instead, it connects us to life more deeply and more passionately.

> *A saint was once asked, while playing happily with his companions, what he would do if an angel told him*

that in a quarter of an hour he would die and have to
appear before the judgment seat of God. The saint
promptly replied that he would continue playing
because I am certain these games are pleasing to
God.—ST. JOHN BOSCO

There's a scene from the life of Francis that I find particularly relevant to the life we live at the Little Portion
community. Francis, a fellow friar, and two younger
novices were walking across a hill on a cold, snowy day.
Without warning, Francis and the two novices were
moved by joy. They began dancing together and then
rolled down the hill together in the snow.

The older brother frowned disapprovingly at this gra-
tuitous display of glee, and later expressed his displeasure
personally to Francis. Francis responded by telling the
friar that joy was an essential part of their communal life,
and warning him that if he didn't develop a capacity for
joy, he wouldn't last long in their community. Soon, just
as Francis had predicted, the brother parted ways with
his fellow Franciscans.

This may come as a shock to some people who've
never visited one, but monasteries are joyful places, not
sad, dreary places. Even though we have our moments of
solemnity, our rituals, and our customs, spontaneity and
an infectious, childlike joy drip like honey from a honey-
comb. In this, we are the glad inheritors of a lengthy
Franciscan tradition.

Let your understanding strengthen your patience. In
serenity look forward to the joy that follows sadness.
—ST. PETER DAMIAN

▨ Cultivating Joy

You don't have to relocate to a monastery to experience joy in your life. And even though joy can't be produced or manufactured, there are things you can do to increase the likelihood that you'll encounter joy in your own life. Here are a few time-tested suggestions.

✠ *Don't Worry about Tomorrow*

James the brother of Jesus was critical of the arrogance of those who tried to control their lives through detailed, far-reaching plans: "You don't even know what will happen tomorrow. What is your life? You are a mist that appears for a little while and then vanishes."

Likewise, in small ways and big ways, Francis sought not to be distracted from the responsibilities of today by worries about tomorrow. When he sent his friars out to collect alms, he instructed them only to collect enough for one day. And he forbade the monastery's friar cooks from soaking vegetables the night before they were to be cooked.

The Jesuit writer Jean Pierre DeCoussaid describes this kind of attention to the here and now as "the sacrament of the present moment." This doesn't mean one can't have plans or hopes for tomorrow. But it does mean that too many of us are too preoccupied about the future—or too consumed by the past—to concentrate on the beauty and the promise of the current.

Embrace the immediate moment. Practice being present when you're washing the dishes, cutting the grass, relaxing in the bath tub, or taking out the trash. Learn how to be alive in the here and now instead of constantly dreaming and scheming for something better.

✝ *Be Thankful*

What's your first waking thought in the morning? Is it a teeth-clenching curse about how cold you are, how tired you are, or how anxious you are about the responsibilities of the coming day? Instead of moaning and groaning, try beginning each day with a prayer of thanks to God for another day of life.

What's your last thought as you lay your head down on your pillow? Is your mind full of static and frustration from a long, harried day? Or are you so tired that you conk out as soon as you get horizontal? Try closing each day with a prayer of thanks to God for the blessings (and trials) of another day.

If you open and close each day with thanks, you might be surprised to find an attitude of thankfulness creeping into the rest of your day as well.

✝ *Be Forgiving*

Many people walk around in a black cloud of their own creation. Part of the cloud consists of regrets over personal failures or unfaithfulness to others. The good news is that God can forgive us for these failings, and give us a clean conscience for starting anew.

But another part of the cloud consists of the emotional bondage we bring on ourselves when we fail to forgive others. We're angry at a coworker about a slight, real or perceived. We resent how a neighbor's dog dirtied our driveway. Or we're peeved at a driver who swerved in front of us on the highway. Sure, intense emotions like these get some people fueled up and energized, but they are also prone to spontaneous combustion, and they can engulf our lives with their deadly flames. Learn to forgive, thus freeing yourself from the illusions of both control and victimization.

True joy is the earnest wish we have of heaven, it is a treasure of the soul, and therefore should be laid in a safe place, and nothing in this world is safe to place it in.—JOHN DONNE

If you wanted your money to make money, you would deposit it in a bank, where it would earn interest. Or you would give it to a broker, who could invest it for you. You wouldn't throw it down a sewer grate, hoping against hope that your money would come back from the sewer with interest.

Likewise, too many of us have spent our lives in unworthy pursuits and have suffered the consequences of sadness, sorrow, and suffering. Instead of setting out on the impossible search for happiness, why not begin seeking joy, which leads to a deeper and more fulfilling way to live.

Begin by saying this simple prayer: "God, my efforts to make myself happy have yielded much unhappiness. My anxiety about my tomorrows steals the pleasure from my todays. And my anger toward my neighbor strangles my heart. Please release me from my preoccupation with myself and my troubles, and begin filling me with your indescribable joy. Amen."

4
Solitude

He would seek out some lonely spot or an abandoned church where he could go to pray at night. —St. Bonaventure

Ponder a pond. On a still day, its surface is like a mirror, reflecting the blueness of the sky, the big, billowy clouds, and the brilliance of the sun. Then, if your eyes penetrate the surface and look into the calm, motionless water, you can see clear down to the bottom, with its rocks and pebbles. Occasionally, a fish or a frog will swim past in this beautiful, translucent pool.

But things change when the pond is disturbed by a rock, a bounding dog, or a group of active children. Sooner than you can say splash, the surface is agitated by ripples, drops, and waves, and the water under the surface is shot through with air bubbles and clouded with mud.

In many ways, our lives are a lot like ponds. When things are calm, you can see clear down to the bottom, and detect the slightest movement and motion. But when things are unsettled, everything's murky and impenetrable. Unfortunately, few of us have lives that are like a still, serene pond. For most of us, life is more like a kitchen blender, its engine humming, its blades purring, and its motion making a puree of the elements of our fast-paced, turbulent lives.

Francis was no hermit. He lived a full and active life surrounded by fellow friars or people in need. But Francis also knew the value of solitude, silence, and stillness. He sought these treasures whenever he could, and they gave his work in the world a grounded stability that made the investment worthwhile. Likewise, our lives will be fuller and more effective if we learn how to practice the quiet virtues of solitude, silence, and stillness.

> *We seem so frightened today of being alone that we never let it happen. . . . We choke the space with continuous music, chatter, and companionship to which we do not even listen. It is simply there to fill the vacuum. When the noise stops there is no inner music to take its place.*—ANNE MORROW LINDBERGH

Monasteries, hermitages, and retreat centers have been created so that people who wanted to hear the still, small voice of God could turn down the deafening and disquieting cacophony of sound coming from a busy, bustling world.

Monastic-type communities exist in all major religious traditions. In the Christian tradition, they developed in the first few centuries A.D. when solitary hermits fled to the desert to commune with God and duke it out with the Devil. Soon, these hermits formed networks for fellowship and mutual support, and the first Christian monasteries were created.

Some of us may wonder what those early monks were fleeing from. After all, wasn't theirs a much quieter time? Jet airplanes didn't crisscross the sky, four-lane thoroughfares didn't cut through their communities, high-watt home entertainment centers and portable boom boxes didn't fill private and public spaces with the continual din of prefabricated cultural commodities, and towns were still relatively small and simple, unlike our modern megalopolises, where growing numbers of houses and apartments are placed right next to—or on top of—each other. But our age, full as it is with jangly distractions, isn't the first to know noise. Even in Francis's time, the disturbing din of the world was never far away.

One day, the pomp (and pomposity) of life's rich pageant passed right by the humble hut where Francis and some of his friars were staying. And Francis, as he often did, turned his back on the spectacle to focus on deeper things. Here's how the early Franciscan biographer Thomas of Celano described it:

> When at that time the Emperor Otto was passing through the place with much clamor and pomp to receive the crown of his earthly empire, the most holy father, who was living with his brothers in that hovel close to the road on which the emperor would pass, did not even go out to watch; and he did not let

anyone else do so except one who continuously called out to the emperor that his glory would last but a short time. For the glorious saint, withdrawn within himself and walking in the broadness of his heart, had prepared within himself a dwelling fit for God, and therefore the outward clamor did not catch his ears, nor could any sound drive out or interrupt the great business he had at hand.

It wasn't that Francis was aloof from the world, or unconcerned about its needs. Far from it. Francis and his followers spent much of their time traveling, serving, and preaching. And even though Francis established nearly two dozen hermitages during his life, these houses of prayer were built just outside of towns, where the friars could be far enough away from the hustle and bustle to meditate and pray but close enough that they could walk to where the people were to serve and minister.

But Francis worked hard to keep the chaos of the world at arm's length, because he knew deep down in his soul that the commotion of the world can confuse us, seduce us, and suck us into a false reality that has little to do with transcendent, eternal values.

Francis saw that the world's noise has a way of deflecting people from the deeper realities of life. It keeps us preoccupied with the superficial at the expense of the meaningful. It deafens our souls and subdues our hearts. For Francis and other saints, monastics, and mystics down through the ages, the desire for solitude isn't an effort to flee from the world; it's an attempt to run toward God, to know God better, and to hear God's voice amid the din.

Or as Cistercian monk Thomas Merton put it, solitude, silence, and stillness help us "recuperate spiritual powers that may have been gravely damaged by the noise and rush of a pressurized existence."

> *Contemplation is nothing else but a secret, peaceful and loving infusion of God, which, if admitted, will set the soul on fire with the Spirit of love.*
> —St. John of the Cross

Solitude seeks to silence a noisy world. But it is also a tool to quiet our souls, which are often wracked by their own inner turmoil, tensions, and troubles.

One thing many people realize when they first participate in retreats at monasteries is how noisy their own minds and hearts are. We continually replay and revise conversations we had with loved ones, a coworker or boss, or a cashier at a convenience store. We worry about the past and fret about the future. We remember things we forgot, and we fill our minds with mental notes designed to keep us from forgetting them again. Our egos wage an unending battle for fragile self-esteem, while our nagging self-doubts make us feel we are unworthy of that esteem, whether from ourselves or from others.

Priest and author Henri Nouwen described the crazy cacophony that can fill the soul of someone seeking silence in a memorable way: "Your inner life is like a banana tree filled with monkeys jumping up and down."

Our inner worlds often resemble a three-ring circus or a noisy carnival instead of a cool, calm, crystal-clear pond.

Francis wasn't the first saint to realize the challenge of finding inner peace and quiet. He met the challenge head on by punctuating his busy schedule with long and luxurious periods of isolation and quiet. And he devised some unique and effective techniques for promoting silence and solitude within Franciscan communities.

In one of his surviving writings, "Religious Life in Hermitages," Francis proposes that some friars act as "mothers," taking care of monastery logistics and maintaining an atmosphere of meditation, while others are to act as "sons," concentrating wholeheartedly on union with God and leaving everything else to Mom!

"The friars who are mothers must be careful to stay away from outsiders and . . . keep their sons away from them, so that no one can speak to them," wrote Francis. "Now and then the sons should exchange places with the mothers, according to whatever arrangement seems best suited for the moment. But they should all be careful to observe what has been laid down for them, eagerly and zealously."

Francis and his godly friars wouldn't have dedicated so much time and energy to finding and protecting silence if it were easy or came naturally. If anything, cultivating solitude has only grown more complicated in the ensuing centuries. But solitude, silence, and stillness remain essential ingredients to the spiritually directed life.

A loss of silence is as serious as a loss of memory and just as disorienting. Silence is, after all, the natural context from which we listen. Silence is also the natural context from which we speak.
—CORNELIUS PLANTINGA, JR.

In all areas of his life, Francis desired to imitate the life of Christ. And like Christ, Francis spent time in solitude with God before embarking on large, public activities or making important decisions about the course his life should take. Francis sought solitude whenever he could, either in prolonged periods of isolation, brief periods of prayer and meditation, or hurried prayers said as he worked and walked in towns and cities.

It may come as a surprise to some people, but solitude, at least as it's practiced by Franciscans, isn't a retreat from the world and its demands. Quite the contrary: In my life, as in Francis's life, solitude is a way of recharging my spiritual batteries for deeper, more effective, and more selfless service to the world and others.

During my life as a Franciscan, first as a lay friar and later as a Brother of Charity, I've recorded dozens of albums, written a dozen books, founded and served as the spiritual father of the Brothers and Sisters of Charity, traveled on musical and speaking tours, and visited foreign countries with Mercy Corps, a Christian humanitarian organization. Like all of us, I sometimes feel I'm too busy, that my life is too crowded and my time too pressed.

Still, I don't know what I would do if I couldn't

spend three to four hours a day in prayer to God. I find that when I'm grounded in silence and prayer, the work I do becomes efficient, energized, and empowered by God's spirit. The more I devote my time to prayer, the more I get done in my periods of activity. But if I focus on spending my time in activity, I quickly realize that I'm getting little done.

Writer Glenn Tinder recently summed up the way solitude can help us balance our "private" and "public" lives. It's a lengthy passage, but a rich one:

> If you have never, all alone, tried to define your major convictions, you cannot enter into truth-seeking conversation and are thus incapable of deep human relations. If you cannot be apart from others, you cannot engage in prayer and meditation and thus cannot enter into genuine relationship with God. If you recoil from solitude, it may even be said, you are politically disabled; you necessarily lack the spirit of independence needed to stand for what is right in the public realm.

It's true: Solitude, silence, and stillness help us connect to God. But God doesn't intend that we take such spiritual riches and keep them to ourselves or hoard them away. Instead, the genius of the Franciscan approach is its balance between quiet meditation and activity in the world. Intimacy with God becomes a prelude to intimacy with and service to others.

Not all men are called to be hermits, but all men need enough silence and solitude in their lives to enable the deep inner voice of their own true self to be heard at least occasionally.—THOMAS MERTON

I have found that the discipline of solitude brings three important benefits:

✤ You know yourself better.
✤ You know God better.
✤ You know your purpose better.

I know solitude has helped me know myself better. In 1978, following a number of turbulent years during which Mason Proffit had disbanded, my marriage had fallen apart, and I had converted to the Catholic faith, I put my musical career on hold and retreated to the woods of Indiana where I built a small hut and adapted a primitive existence of poverty, humility, manual labor, and rich, deep solitude.

I found someone willing to give me old stones and bricks which, after I cleaned them, worked quite well for my walls. I converted some old oil drums into a wood-burning heater. I sewed a primitive Franciscan habit out of a few old army blankets. And I worked as a gardener for a nearby retreat house, which provided me with the basics of food and water.

During the months I spent in my little hut, I learned much about the cycles of nature, I became more acquainted with the ways of numerous squirrels and other animal neighbors, and I immersed myself in the teachings of Jesus and the writings of saints and sages.

But more than anything, I learned things about myself that I never knew before.

Unfortunately, not everything I saw in myself was good. It's like looking into a clear pond: sometimes you'll see rocks and fish in the water. But lurking in the shallows may be old shoes, used tires, discarded cans, and various pieces of garbage. And it was this refuse that I often saw when I looked deep into myself. I saw a man who was in many ways a child, and who had failed as a son, a husband, a father, and a follower of Jesus.

Through large doses of God's love and grace, I received significant forgiveness and healing for much of the debris in my life. It wasn't like I persuaded myself that all the dirt in my life was really diamonds. Instead, I became aware that God loved me in spite of my unloveliness. And that soothing, challenging grace helped me confront my demons and begin my life anew.

It's been nearly twenty years since my solitary months in those quiet Indiana woods. I'll never forget the things I learned there, and how I went beyond the superficial aspects of my personality and my "talents" to the deep center of my being. And one of the ways I stay in touch with my deeper self is through regular periods of solitude and silence.

Your mind should be full of love of God, forgetful of yourself.—Venerable Charles de Foucauld

Solitude, silence, and stillness also help you know God better. Biographies of Francis are full of passages like this one, from St. Bonaventure's *Minor Life*, which describes Francis's desire to seek out a private and intimate setting where he could commune with God:

> Here, in hidden secrecy, he defended himself before his Judge; here he pleaded with his Father; here he enjoyed the company of his divine Bridegroom; here he spoke with his Lover.

In the Christian tradition, one of the central episodes of the history of the human race is the Fall, that watershed event recorded early in the Old Testament book of Genesis when Adam and Eve trade in a pretty good deal—a sinless life and perfect union with God—for a much inferior package: attempting to be like God by eating of the tree of the knowledge of good and evil.

Before the Fall, the first man and woman had a natural disposition toward transparent living and a common-sense dependence on God. But after the Fall, they no longer sought out God to commune with him, but fled from God to escape divine displeasure and judgment. Adam and Eve hid from God, and by and large, most of us have been hiding from God ever since.

Solitude is one way to reveal yourself to God and invite God to dwell within you and reveal himself to you. In the desert of Judah, David composed a psalm that expressed his yearning for a union with God:

> O God, you are my God,
> earnestly I seek you;
> my soul thirsts for you,
> in a dry and weary land
> where there is no water.

There's nothing magical about solitude that makes God suddenly appear. God is everywhere all the time. It's just that most of the time we are so busy with everything else that we don't notice. But by practicing the discipline of solitude, we are creating a space in our lives where God can be with us. And over time, as that space grows, so can our relationship with the living God.

> *Prayer reveals to souls the vanity of earthly goods and pleasures. It fills them with light, strength and consolation, and gives them a foretaste of the calm bliss of our heavenly home.*—St. Rose of Viterbo

Spending time alone with God can also help you better know your purpose in life. After all, God created you and knows best what you're supposed to do with your life. But beyond that, solitude helps protect you from the consequences of the dreaded twin evils that bedevil most everything we do: failure and success.

We all know how failure can hurt. You imagine something, plan it, create it, and unveil it before the waiting world. And then the jeers begin, shocking you and forcing you back into your hole, and making you think twice before you ever create anything again. In the midst of such potentially life-shattering disapproval, intimacy with God can help you ride out these rough spots, remembering that God loves you and values you for more than what you do.

God can also help us deal with the dizzying dangers of success. Suppose you unveil your masterpiece and the crowd goes wild? While some people may have the internal fortitude to continue following the muse and doing what they're supposed to do, others are unduly swayed by the approval and the applause. The applause becomes more important than the creative act, and wanting to remain popular and loved, we begin to change what we do to play to the crowd. We go for ratings rather than for what we know is right.

Intimacy with God, which can only be attained through the disciplines of solitude, silence, and stillness, helps us to avoid being detoured by popular acclaim.

Some people threw stones at Francis, calling him a lunatic. Others hailed him as a "second Christ." But he didn't let either the scorn or the praise turn his head; the lepers, the lowly, and the outcasts were his focus, not the powerful people of his time. Likewise, some hailed Jesus as the redeemer of Israel and wanted to make him a king. Others hurled insults and spat at him, and it was some of these people who ultimately crucified him. I don't know about you, but if I were planning a career, having my life end in a gruesome death on a cross wouldn't seem like success. But Jesus kept his heart set on the mission before him, redeeming the world through the suffering and the weakness he endured.

When it's all said and done, it isn't the world's

commendation or its condemnation that let us know how well we've done in life. It's the approval of God communicated in the depths of our hearts. And only solitude, regularly practiced and deeply lived, can help keep us on that path.

> *No one can approach God without withdrawing from the world.*—ST. ISAAK OF SYRIA

Quiet doesn't just happen. You have to cultivate it and provide places for it to blossom. At Little Portion, we do that through a schedule that guides the life of our community and alternates periods of silence and action.

Our day begins at 6:45 A.M. with a service of morning prayer and communion. This service includes readings from the Gospels and periods of singing as well as times of silent meditation. We then have a silent breakfast, during which we try not to speak very much unless it's really necessary. Generally during this period, there is some conversation in quiet tones, which doesn't disturb the overall mood of silence. This kind of silence continues until noon, after which everyone is free to speak in a normal voice.

The quietest period at Little Portion is something we call the Grand Silence, which goes from 10 P.M. until our morning service. During the hours of the Grand Silence, we don't speak and we try not to make noises that would disturb the others.

Other communities or monasteries have their own schedules and ways of creating a space for solitude and quiet. Some are very rigorous and allow very little sound at all. But for us, our approach is balanced, flexible, and practical, and it allows those among us who are seeking silent communion with God to do so without being overly rigid.

> *Do not be disturbed by the clamor of the world which passes like a shadow. Do not let the false delights of a deceptive world deceive you.*—St. Clare of Assisi

You may not have the desire or the liberty to join a community where silence is practiced as part of the daily schedule. But solitude isn't just for monks! Everyone needs it, perhaps especially those people who function in the midst of our big, bustling world. Here are some suggestions for finding moments of hushed serenity in the midst of noise.

One of the most important things you can do is to find a place where you can practice solitude and stillness. If you're near a park that has a bench or a spot for a portable chair, that might work. But some outdoor spaces are noise magnets and not very helpful for prayer and meditation. A place that has too much activity might prove distracting, and a place with too many people might inhibit you from opening your heart to God. Such a place would never do for Francis, who "sought out a quiet and secret place of solitude," and frequented "secluded spots" where "he poured out his whole soul with groans beyond all utterance."

If public spaces won't work, you may need to make room in your house or apartment. Just about any part of your house will do, but make sure it's a space that gives you seclusion, and that it's a place set aside for the purpose of being silent and still. For most people, kitchens and family rooms often don't work because they're too cluttered, or because they contain too many reminders of all the other more "practical" things you think you ought to be doing. That's hardly a recipe for quietness. Instead, your quiet place should be as uncluttered as you want your soul to be!

Some people create a special corner in a room, which they decorate with plants or flowers, paintings or sacred images, or a simple cross. If you're in a noisy apartment, you may also want to invest in a small indoor fountain, whose bubbling water will remind you of nature and mask noises from your neighbors. Or you may want to get some compact discs of calm, soothing, meditative music that can obscure other sounds and help you to still yourself. I know people whose meditation areas are stocked with CDs of classical or ambient music, or Gregorian chant.

One thought on distraction: Don't get hung up on finding the perfect environment. It doesn't exist! Instead, make your distractions part of your prayer experience. If someone slams a door, pray that God will bless that person wherever they go, then return to your meditations. If someone's car alarm goes off, ask God to protect them as they drive. Or, as the anonymous author of the medieval mystical guide *The Cloud of Unknowing* put it, picture distractions coming at you like floating objects, then move your head and let them pass, continuing to focus on God and your own internal quietness.

Instead of concentrating on all the sounds around you and being overwhelmed by them, learn to build a foundation of internal silence that prevents you from being distracted.

> *In our culture, time can seem like an enemy: It chews us up and spits us out with appalling ease. But the monastic perspective welcomes time as a gift from God, and seeks to put it to good use, rather than allowing us to be used up by it.*
> —KATHLEEN NORRIS

If you're like many Americans, finding a solitary space may be easier than finding the time in your schedule for solitude. But if you want your life to be built around things that are truly important rather than things that are simply urgent, you've got to take positive steps. And the only way to be absolutely certain that solitude happens is to schedule it.

The beginning and the end of the day are popular times to seek solitude. Often, they're quieter than other times of the day, and they allow you to pray and reflect on the day ahead, or the day just completed. But others find more success with a midday prayer walk that allows them to leave the house or the office for a few moments of focused, intentional meditation.

Quiet times can also be family times, as they are in monasteries around the world. Try involving your spouse or children in brief times of community solitude. Begin by having someone read a brief passage from the Bible or an inspiring story or quote. Then be silent together, perhaps interspersing your silence with prayers for family members or others.

And while we're talking about time, see if you can schedule more intense periods of solitude on a weekly, monthly, and yearly basis. Perhaps you can have a longer period of silence on Sundays, the day on which the earliest Christians met, to recharge yourself for the coming week. In addition, maybe you can spend half a day a month in more intensive prayer and fasting. And many people try to schedule at least one prayer retreat for a weekend or longer at one of the hundreds of monasteries or retreat centers that offer such programs. I'm sure you'll be able to find a facility near you that offers spiritual guidance, which may prove helpful if you're new at this.

> *The soul that is growing in holiness is the least lonely when it is most alone.*—FATHER ANDREW

The months I spent in my tiny hut in Indiana helped break my addiction to hustle and bustle. But sometimes it seems as if dozens of people are rushing to occupy the spot on the crazy roller coaster that I exited. I wonder if many of the world's most avid noise makers and consumers of noise aren't actually afraid of what they would find deep down inside if they ever got alone in silence with themselves and with God.

Don't run from silence. Accept God's gracious invitation to the joys of solitude. Don't fill your days with noxious noise, or your nights with a constant stream of unfunny sitcoms, boring adventure flicks, or prefabricated pop music.

I invite you to step into the calm, cool water of silence and seek God there. Or as Henri Nouwen has written, "To live a spiritual life we must first find the courage to enter the desert of our loneliness and to change it by gentle and persistent efforts into a garden of solitude."

5

Humility

❧

Brother Francis, the least of your servants, worthless and sinful, sends greetings.

—FRANCIS

LIFELESS AND WATERLESS, THE MOON IS a pale reflection of the solar system's brightly shining main attraction. But so far as we know, the moon has never objected to its supporting role in the cosmos or staged a walkout over its dependent status.

Instead, the floating mass of rock and minerals Francis called Sister Moon seems quite content to brilliantly illumine the darkened sky by reflecting the hidden light of the sun. And we marvel at its looming, luminescent presence, which has cast its light on millions of romances, inspired both science fiction films and real-life explorations, and served as a close and constant reminder of the mysteries and vastness of space.

You and I can learn a valuable lesson from Sister Moon. Like her, we're not the focus of the universe— even though we sometimes act like it. Amid the immensity and grandeur of the cosmos, we are small and dependent beings whose chief glory is to reflect God's brilliance.

At least that's the way things are supposed to be. But too often, our pride gets in the way, causing needless pain and sorrow for ourselves and for others while preventing us from being what God intended.

Francis had a keen understanding of the power and danger of human pride, and he condemned it as spiritual enemy number one. Like other saints before him, he knew the only way to disarm the vice of pride was through the ceaseless practice of the virtue of humility.

Francis, perhaps the most humble person the world has ever known, expressed his belief in "The Praises of the Virtues":

> Holy Humility puts pride to shame,
> and all the inhabitants of this world
> and all that is in the world.

The gate of Heaven is very low; only the humble can enter it.—ST. ELIZABETH SETON

God brings the proud low. That's what happened to Lucifer, the once-beautiful angel who wanted a bigger piece of the action, rebelled against God, and was expelled from heaven. And it was pride that made Adam and Eve want to become like God, eat the forbidden fruit, and turn their back on their creator. In the Christian tradition, this is called the Original Sin, or the Fall. But all major faiths have their own concept of this malignancy at the heart of creation, this sense that everything's slightly askew.

Over millennia of human history, pride has ceased to be original any longer, functioning much the same way today as it did in the Garden of Eden: deluding us into thinking that we'll be happier going our own way, erecting barriers between ourselves and God and putting up walls of competition, suspicion, and distrust between ourselves and our brothers and sisters.

Pride inflates our egos and desires, making us insist on getting what we want in the world instead of trying to live out the message of the Lord's prayer: "Your will be done, on earth as it is in heaven." And if left unchecked, pride is a cancer that takes over our souls and ultimately leads to death.

Francis would have nothing to do with it, as St. Bonaventure wrote in his *Major Life* of Francis: "The saint had a horror of pride, which is the cause of all evil, and of disobedience, which was its worst offspring."

Francis saw that the only antidote to pride is humility. It was for prideful people such as me that Francis articulated a way of life that takes pride seriously and takes steps to minimize its destructive influence. And the cornerstone of this way of life is a clear-eyed comprehension of our utter dependence on God.

People in Alcoholics Anonymous and other Twelve Step groups are urged to take a look at the mess they've made of their lives and ask for help from a "Higher Power." This process is essential to breaking an addiction to alcohol, but it's also required if we are to break our dysfunctional addiction to pride.

As Francis saw it, breaking the bondage of pride required nothing less than conversion, or more precisely, a lifelong series of conversions—some small and insignificant, some devastating and earthshaking. Through these daily conversions, God leads us by the hand and shows us again and again that we're not God, only God is.

> *The only way to make rapid progress along the path of divine love is to remain very little and put all our trust in Almighty God.*—St. Thérèse of Lisieux

Walk through a bookstore's business section and you'll see rack after rack of books praising the values of aggressiveness, competition, self-centeredness, and confidence. But Francis lived and preached a radical message of downward mobility: littleness, humbleness, submission, obedience, and service. Every time, Francis chose poverty over wealth, powerlessness over power, and serving over ruling.

The small chapel where Francis's movement got its start was called the Portiuncula, which means "little portion." (That's where our Little Portion Hermitage in Arkansas gets its name.) When the movement had grown and it came time for Francis to give a name to the ragtag group that was following him and dedicating themselves to his mission, he chose a title that speaks volumes: "I wish that this fraternity should be called the Order of Friars Minor," he said. If we can understand just a little about the world of Francis's day, we will see how revolutionary his insistence on being "minor" truly is.

Thirteenth-century Europe was being transformed from a rural, agrarian society based on barter to an increasingly urban culture based on cash. At the same time, people sought higher social standing. Serfs sought to become free peasants, peasants sought to become part of an emerging middle class, and members of the middle class sought to become part of the increasingly powerful noble class. Everyone was trying, through legal and illegal means, to make the leap from the *minores* (or common people) to the *majores* (the great, or the nobility). And a few, such as Francis's father, succeeded.

But just as his family and much of Europe's populace was relentlessly striving upward and onward, Francis said true joy and real greatness came from striving downward. To Francis, bigger wasn't better, smaller was. Or as he wrote: "It is not for us to be wise and calculating in the world's fashion; we should be guileless, lowly, and pure." Francis rigorously followed the way of humility and instructed his followers to do the same.

Francis forbade his friars from accepting positions of power and authority. When a bishop approached Francis about promoting some of the Franciscan friars to offices in the church, Francis was shocked. "My lord," Francis replied, "my friars are called Minors so that they will never think of becoming superiors. If you want them to bear fruit in the church, keep them strictly to their vocation and never let them take any office in the church."

Later, Francis asked God to keep his movement humble: "I pray you, therefore, Father, that you by no means permit them to rise to any prelacy, lest they become prouder rather than poorer and grow arrogant toward the rest."

Do nothing out of selfish ambition or vain conceit, but in humility consider others better than your-selves.—St. Paul

One of the best tests of a person's humility is to see how he or she treats others. St. Paul tells us to consider others as better than ourselves. But how do we do that? Doesn't that lead to a false humility?

Here at Little Portion there is a brother named Bob who plays guitar at some of our services. Most people would agree that Bob is an average guitarist, which is fine, because he's not interested in performing at concerts or winning awards at international competitions. His goal is helping us sing simple worship songs, which he does just fine.

But for me, playing guitar is my craft, my ministry, and my career. I spend hours in practice. I discipline myself to work on difficult chords and runs until I can play them with seeming effortlessness. It would not be "humility" for me to tell Bob that he's a better guitarist in order to "consider him better than myself." It would be dishonesty.

On the other hand, Bob is a dear brother with a gentle heart and a sincere compassion for others. In fact, he's much more sensitive to the needs of others than I often am. I respect him for that, and consider him better than me in that area of his life.

Humility allows me to appreciate Bob and others in our community for their unique personalities, talents, and gifts. One sister gives herself selflessly to others in need. One brother is a talented sculptor who labors to create works of beauty on our property. Another is a talented gardener who can coax luxurious fruits and vegetables out of a simple plot of ground. One is a devoted mystic who spends hours in prayer adoring God and praying for the sorrows of the world. Another is a master veterinarian, bringing sick animals back to health and happiness with his unique combination of potions and barn-side manner.

I may be the best guitarist in our community, but we would starve real soon if others didn't sustain us with their gifts, their unique abilities, and their willingness to serve the community. Playing guitar doesn't give me the right to be puffed up and arrogant about the abilities God has given me. And it doesn't give me the right to run down other people whose gifts are in other areas.

If you should ask me what are the ways of God, I would tell you that the first is humility, the second is humility, and the third is still humility. Not that there are no other precepts to give, but if humility does not precede all that we do, our efforts are fruitless.
—St. Augustine

Nothing keeps one humble like self-awareness. I am acutely conscious of my own egotism and the blackness that can dwell at the center of my soul. But when I'm tempted to despair, I'm comforted by the words of Francis, who though he was revered by many as a saint, never forgot that he was a sinner: "I have sinned in many ways, through my own most grievous fault, and in particular by not keeping the Rule which I promised to God, and by not saying the Office, as the Rule prescribes, through carelessness or sickness, or because I am ignorant and have never studied."

Francis was not a pessimist or a perpetual malcontent bent on making himself and those around him miserable and insecure. But he did see a huge spiritual chasm separating the goodness of God from the evil of humanity.

Today, many people are uncomfortable with talk about human evil. They believe such talk is injurious to healthy self-esteem and should have been left in the Middle Ages. Francis would disagree, but he balanced his comments on human frailty with poetic praise of human dignity. Alluding to opening chapters of the book of Genesis, he said, "Try to realize the dignity God has conferred on you. He created and formed your body in the image of his beloved Son, and your soul in his own likeness."

Some people are very skeptical about the possibility for human redemption. But Francis would prefer to see humanity as a dust-covered mirror: designed to reflect God's glory, but too dirty to do the job. For me, the good news is that God does windows! His love can clean us, purify us, and make us creatures of spiritual beauty.

We are both sinful and spiritual, both frail and dignified. Understanding this balance helps us remain humble and allows us to have healthy self-esteem without slipping into egotism.

What was the life of Christ but a perpetual humiliation?—St. Vincent de Paul

Francis's emphasis on humility sprang from his desire to imitate the humility of Christ, whose life was framed by two episodes of supreme humility. In the Incarnation, he emptied himself of his divinity to be born in human form and walk among us. In the Crucifixion, he gave up his life for a sinful world. In between his birth and his death, Jesus served the poor and the needy, washed the feet of his disciples, urged those who wished to follow him to sit in the lowliest place at the table, and preached a message of redemption for the world: "Come to me, all you who are weary and burdened, and I will give you rest. Take my yoke upon you and learn from me, for I am gentle and humble in heart, and you will find rest for your souls."

Francis referred to the humility of Christ's ministry as "the condescension of God." And part of why Francis loved to celebrate the Eucharist, or Mass, was because this sacrament of the church was a clear reenactment of this divine humility: "What wonderful majesty! What stupendous condescension! O sublime humility! O humble sublimity! That the Lord of the whole universe, God and the Son of God, should humble himself like this and hide under the form of a little bread, for our salvation."

When Francis looked at Jesus, he saw the creator of the universe come down to be born in a smelly stable for the love of you and me. In his desire to be more like Jesus, Francis determined that smallness should be a big part of his life.

> *I find the doing of the will of God leaves me no time for disputing about His plans.*
> —George MacDonald

Francis believed that humility would result in obedience, and that obedience was a prerequisite to knowing and doing the will of God.

Whenever I speak in public about the subject of obedience, I can hear a collective groan rise from the audience.

Americans worship individualism and demand independence from governmental or religious control. Mention the word *obedience* and people conjure up images of an abusive religious cult or a nun or a priest rapping students' knuckles with a ruler.

The Italy of Francis's time shared some of our distaste for submission to religious authorities. The church had become involved in affairs of state, it had grown decadent, and its message carried a hollow ring. Throughout the Middle Ages, a series of self-proclaimed reformers and prophets appeared on the scene, broke off from the church, and created their own autonomous movements.

People have portrayed Francis as a religious revolutionary, but he was a loyal member and servant of the church. Francis could have easily gone his own way, but he didn't. As soon as he had more than a handful of followers, he went to see the pope to receive the church's blessing and guidance. True, Francis was an outspoken critic of hypocritical and power-hungry leaders, be they religious or secular. But still he respected the centuries of Christian tradition and the spiritual authority in the church. Francis was a radical reformer but not an iconoclastic crusader. And his obedience and commitment helped bring rivers of renewal into the church of his day.

Francis also practiced obedience in his personal life. As soon as the Franciscan Order was established, he resigned from its leadership and became simply another of the friars. Furthermore, he placed himself under the authority of a series of brothers, most of whom were much younger in years and in the faith than he. He wrote: "Among the other things the kindness of God has generously granted me, it has granted me this grace that I would obey a novice of one hour, if he were given me as my guardian, as carefully as I would obey the oldest and most discreet person."

Francis's life was governed by a divine dispassion, a holy detachment. He remained calm and humble, grounded in God's grace, no matter the winds that howled around him.

> *Father, I abandon myself into Your hands; do with me what You will. I am ready for all, I accept all.*
> —VENERABLE CHARLES DE FOUCAULD

Children hate embarrassment, and adolescents flee humiliation like the plague. But Francis found exaltation in humiliation. Instead of avoiding humbling experiences, Francis sought them out, and often in ways that may seem extreme to us now. As he wrote in his Rule, "I entreat all my friars, whether they are given to preaching, praying, or manual labor, to do their best to humble themselves at every opportunity."

Francis was leery of the adulation of crowds, and his built-in pride detector went into action when he was praised by others, which happened often. Thomas of Celano and other biographers tell of the saint's many efforts to remain humble:

> For often, when he was honored by all, he suffered the deepest sorrow; and rejecting the favor of men, he would see to it that he would be rebuked by someone. He would call some brother to him, saying to him: "In obedience, I say to you, revile me harshly and speak the truth against the lies of these others." And

when that brother, though unwilling, would say that he was a boor, a hired servant, a worthless being, Francis, smiling and applauding very much, would reply: "May the Lord bless you, for you have spoken most truly."

Likewise, he encouraged his friars to be vigilant. Once when the friars were ridiculed while begging for alms, he encouraged them to beg even more humbly and share in the humiliations of Jesus, who was mocked and crucified. Brother Bernard, one of the first followers of Francis, learned these lessons well. When a group of citizens jeered and made fun of him for his impoverished appearance, "he deliberately went to the public square of the city and sat down so that people would have a better opportunity to make fun of him."

Francis also found that living in community provides plenty of opportunities to experience humility. In our community we've had doctors and lawyers who forgo the privileges of rank on the "outside world" to live together with everyone else and do manual chores. The discipline of monastic life can be extremely humbling, but also extremely ennobling.

> *Francis did his utmost to encourage the friars to lead austere lives, but he had no time for exaggerated self-denial.*—St. Bonaventure

Francis was legendary for punishing his own body and bringing it into submission to his will. He often disparagingly referred to his body as "Brother Ass," and he whipped it as some would a stubborn animal. In many ways, Francis was a product of his times, reflecting the penitential practices of many monastics of his day. When he feared his body was leading his heart away from God, he would wear a hair shirt, stand in the rain, jump into a mound of snow, or find other ways to punish himself.

Undoubtedly, Francis's harshness toward his own body contributed to his poor health and his early death, a fact that he admitted late in his life and for which he expressed regret. But just as he was hard on himself, he was gentle with others. And he cautioned his friars against undue fasts and vigils.

> *Satan fears and trembles before humble souls.*
> —PADRE PIO

You don't have to scourge your body or enter into a monastery to grow in humility. The opportunities to learn humility are all around us. Here are some ways to take stock of the pride in your life and confront it with the discipline of humility:

✤ When you are around other people, do you insist on promoting your opinions, driving home your points, and being the last one to talk on an issue? Or are you content to let others have their say without any commentary or criticism from you?

✤ How do you feel about the driver who cuts you off on the freeway? Are you shocked by his insensitivity to your rights as a driver? Or how do you feel about the family which grabs the restaurant table that you had eyed for yourself? Or what do you feel about the handicapped person who forces you to walk more slowly or delays your ascent up a flight of stairs to an important meeting? Do you easily get bent out of shape and angry about slight inconveniences?

✤ How do you treat others? How do you relate to the person taking your order at the fast food restaurant drive-through window? Are you brusque and insolent? Or how do you interact with the cashier at the local convenience store? Are you all business, or do you have time to exchange a smile, share a word of encouragement, or offer a compliment? Do you demand polite service or are you thankful for it?

How we treat others, particularly others who we view as somehow less important than ourselves, is a crucial test of our humility. One of the first steps in Francis's life of faith was to kiss a leper. Who are the lepers in our lives, and how can we kiss them?

Pride makes us hate our equals because they are our equals; our inferiors for fear that they may equal us; our superiors because they are above us.

—St. John Vianney

Your friends win a free Caribbean cruise. Are you happy for them or are you upset that it didn't happen to you? A coworker gets a promotion. You congratulate her, but are you really angry because you thought you deserved it? A friend who sometimes competes with you in your profession wins a coveted award. Are you glad for his success or afraid that you will lose business?

Blessed is the person who can share the joy of the joyful. Or as Francis put it, blessed is the person "who takes no more pride in the good God says and does through him, than in that which he says and does through someone else."

It's a big world, folks, and there are plenty of goodies to go around for all of us. Don't be stingy. If you're so busy clawing and scratching for every blessing you can squeeze out of life, you won't have time to appreciate the blessings that others receive. Lighten up, loosen up, and find ways to appreciate everyone else's uniqueness and giftedness without viewing this as some kind of criticism of you and the way you are.

A humble man is never hurried, hasty or perturbed, but at all times remains calm. Nothing can ever surprise, disturb or dismay him, for he suffers neither fear nor change in tribulations, neither surprise nor elation in enjoyment. All his joy and gladness are in what is pleasing to the Lord.—St. Isaak of Syria

Pray that you can experience the joy that comes from putting your life in God's hands and being a humble servant. If your life brings riches and fame, thank God. If you get simple circumstances, thank God.

Life gives all of us plenty of surprises. Things rarely turn out as we planned. We need to learn to bend or we will surely break. Humbly embrace what God gives you, and rejoice in what God gives others, as well.

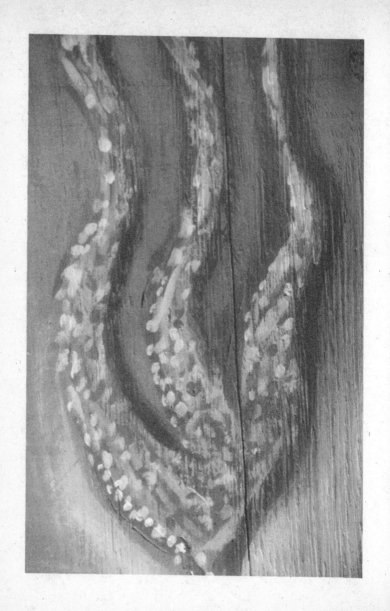

6
Creativity

❧ *Francis sought occasion to love God in everything. In everything beautiful, he saw him who is beauty itself.*

— St. Bonaventure

Monks get a bad rap. Many people assume they live lives of darkness, dreariness, and drudgery. The common misperception is that to be really, really religious means being really, really boring. And after all, isn't a monk's day so full of prayers, rituals, and manual labor that there's no time left for enjoying life? And by the way, doesn't religion teach that it's a sin to enjoy life, or anything else?

Sorry, but Francis's life confounds the idea that being godly means being aesthetically challenged. In addition to praying and preaching, Francis composed poems and songs, staged dramas, and did painting and sculpture. His life has inspired painters, composers, and other artists to soar to new creative heights. The life-affirming vibrancy at the heart of the Franciscan movement helped launch the cornucopia of creativity known as the Renaissance, and the various Franciscan orders have attracted some of the world's best-known artists to their ranks, including the poet Dante, the painter Michelangelo, and the composer Franz Liszt.

Francis wasn't the first artistic monk. Monasteries have long been cradles of creativity and scholarship. In fact, monasticism kept the creativity of Western civilization alive during the Dark Ages. But Francis was exceptionally creative, and he had a visionary way of looking at everyday life. He was enraptured by the splendor and loveliness of the created world, and he was an ardent admirer of goodness everywhere that it could be found. One poet who studied the saint's life and poetry got it right when he said, "though the saint was sworn to poverty, he did not forswear beauty."

His life was a seamless garment of praise for the Creator and joy in the beauty of creativity. Often when he was deep in mystical rapture, Francis would hear the sounds of music. *The Little Flowers of St. Francis* tells us that once the saint was deep in meditation when "all of a sudden an angel appeared to him in a very bright light, holding a viol in his left hand and a bow in his right hand. And as St. Francis gazed in amazement at the angel, the latter drew the bow once upward across the viol. And immediately such a beautiful melody invaded St. Francis' soul and suspended all his bodily senses."

St. Bonaventure tells of another such episode: "One night as he lay awake thinking about God, he suddenly heard the sound of a lyre playing a melody of incredible beauty. With his spirit all intent on God, Francis felt such pleasure at the wonderful melody that he thought he had left this world and the friars who were closest to him were well aware that something had happened."

Toward the end of his life Francis experienced the most lofty spiritual experience ever, the reception of the stigmata, which were physical wounds on his hands, feet, and side matching the wounds Christ received at the Crucifixion. Still pulsing with the spiritual excitement of this mystical encounter, Francis grabbed paper and pen and wrote a poem called "Praises of God." The original copy of this poem is preserved in the Basilica of St. Francis in Assisi, and it includes this line of praise to God: "You are beauty."

It may seem ironic to some that a man whose life was a ceaseless discipline in everything ascetic would find his senses overflowing with all things aesthetic. But probe beneath the surface of his life and you'll see that there's no conflict between Francis's love for the Creator and his experience of creativity. Quite the contrary: The two worked together harmoniously and beautifully.

[Creativity] is a little like opening the gate at the top of a field irrigation system. Once we remove the blocks, the flow moves in.—JULIA CAMERON

You may find this surprising, but one of the things that I find most discomforting about performing my music is how some people look at me like I'm some kind of celebrity. Too many people tend to think that humanity is divided into two groups: the creative people (usually wealthy and attractive types who perform music, or make blockbuster movies, or paint masterpieces) and the rest of us. Such thinking would have troubled Francis, who taught that creativity came with humanity.

In fact, Francis believed that all of us were created to create.

Creativity started with God, who made the entire cosmos out of nothing, populated it with a dizzying variety of plants and animals, and finished it off by producing the first human beings. But a careful reading of the opening chapter of Genesis reveals that God did something unique with humanity:

> God created man in his own image,
> in the image of God he created him;
> male and female he created them.

Unlike animals and plants, which also bear God's traces, humans are created in God's image. And part of what that means is that humans share a unique portion of God's divine, creative spark.

Unfortunately, many people don't necessarily think of themselves as creative beings. In part, that's due to churches that tell people to live according to strict rules of conduct, parents who snuff out their children's creative urges by telling them to grow up and get real, and schools that focus on producing graduates who can make a practical living instead of "daydreaming" or "fantasizing" about being artists. It's no surprise that after a lifetime of such input many of us conclude we're not creative. We come to believe the lie that the creative people are always the *other* people, those who get paid to make art, music, and literature.

One of the most popular recent books on human creativity is *The Artist's Way* by Julia Cameron. Cameron, who gives seminars on unleashing creativity, refers to

God as "the Great Creator" and says the secret of unleashing human creativity lies in "an experience of the mystical union" with God. As she says, "Creativity is God's gift to us. Using our creativity is our gift back to God."

I have similarly thought of God as "The Master Musician": We are his instruments. He gently plucks the strings of our lives to make a harmonious song for all creation. We are like a beautifully crafted guitar, formed, seasoned, and brought to expression by the same hand.

Perhaps as you read this chapter you can begin examining the negative attitudes that have served to block your creative abilities. Maybe a fresh, new perspective will help you open the gates and let the waters of creativity flow onto the dry, parched ground of your life.

> *Do not wonder that I am so religious. An artist who is not could not have produced anything like this. Have we not examples enough in Beethoven, Bach, Raphael and many others?*—ANTONÍN DVOŘÁK

Like many people who have attempted to walk in the footsteps of Francis I have been attracted to the love affair this man of God had with the arts. I may be even more interested in this aspect of the saint's life because I, like Francis, was a musician before my conversion to Christianity. I was a singer in a popular country rock band. Francis was a troubadour who fashioned himself after the French poets who would travel the countryside and sing their courtly love songs.

After I began to follow Jesus, my musical muse didn't dry up and die. Instead, the music I created began to reflect my newfound faith. Where before I had railed like an angry prophet against racism, militarism, and environmental degradation, my new spiritual perspective helped me see that these social ills were all aspects of our separation from God.

After Francis began to imitate the life of Jesus, he too incorporated his creative spark in his new life. The man who had once paraded through the streets of Assisi singing the songs of the troubadours now traveled through the same streets with a group of singing friars.

Francis called his new band of bards the "jongleurs de Dieu." Jongleurs were usually jesters or jugglers who entertained people by bringing a moment of comic relief. (Think of them as a medieval version of the Flying Karamazov Brothers.) Far from turning into a Christian curmudgeon, the man who once belted out songs of chivalric and courtly love now spread the joy of God by becoming a jester of God.

This unique and creative approach to the Christian faith was to characterize the rest of Francis's life, which was marked by tremendous bursts of creativity in the midst of tiring travels, ceaseless preaching, challenging administrative duties, and lengthy periods of isolation and prayer.

The most famous of Francis's many creations is "The Canticle of Brother Sun," a piece which he wrote in 1225 and which is still regularly sung in churches around the world today. Taking his cue from the psalmist David, who said, "The heavens declare the glory of God," Francis crafted a poem that pays homage to the glories of creation: Brother Sun, Sister Moon, Brothers Wind and Air, Sister Water, Brother Fire, and

Sister Earth, our mother. Finally, as proof that his creativity went beyond facile sentimentality, Francis sang the praises of Sister Death, whom he would meet in person the following year.

"The Canticle of Brother Sun" is considered by many critics as the oldest extant poem in any modern language. And part of what made the poem unique was that Francis composed it in his native Umbrian dialect instead of Latin, which was then the official language of poetry and literature. His other poetic works include "Praises of God" and "The Praises of the Virtues."

As we have noted, Francis also created what is generally regarded as the first Christmas manger scene at Greccio, and he is said to have produced other religious dramas, thus popularizing a form that would become the medieval version of our mass-media entertainments like movies and television.

Many poems, letters, and exhortations to his friars that Francis wrote still exist. I only wish we had a recording of one of the many Masses at which Francis sang the Gospel and delivered one of his famous sermons, which one writer described as "sharp arrows which were shot from the bow of divine wisdom and pierced the hearts of everyone."

> *Music's only purpose should be for the glory of God and the recreation of the human spirit.*
> —JOHANN SEBASTIAN BACH

One day one of the friars approached Francis in his retreat at Mount La Verna and asked for his help. The brother was troubled by temptation beyond his strength to resist, and sought Francis's help in resisting the evil.

"Bring me some paper and ink," Francis told the friar, "for I want to write down the words of the Lord and his praises which I have meditated upon in my heart."

As the friar watched, Francis scribbled out thirty-four lines of verse describing various aspects of the character of God, reading in part:

> You are love,
> You are wisdom.
> You are humility,
> You are endurance.
> You are rest,
> You are peace.
> You are joy and gladness.
> You are justice and moderation.
> You are all our riches,
> And you suffice for us.

The poem worked like a doctor's prescription in relieving the friar's moral maladies: "Immediately every temptation was put to flight, and the writing was kept and afterwards it worked wonderful things."

This episode shows the power that good art has to heal and revive us spiritually. Our God-given creativity can help us see God. One of the clearest examples of this kind of spiritual art is icons, the painted representations of Jesus and saints that are used in churches and homes because they are seen as windows into eternal truths that often escape our attention. In the Eastern Orthodox tradition, painting icons is seen as a ministry within the church.

In a similar way, I hope my music is a musical icon, using words and melodies to help listeners find a doorway into the divine. My goal is that they let the music's mystical power transport them to an experience of God's mystery and love. What a joy it is to participate in such an exchange!

Such moments were frequent occurrences for Francis, as a lovely passage from St. Bonaventure's *Minor Life* reveals: "Francis sought occasion to love God in everything. In everything beautiful, he saw him who is beauty itself. . . . He seemed to perceive a divine harmony in the interplay of powers and faculties given by God to his creatures and like the prophet David he exhorted them all to praise God."

Another biography records the saint creating a poem and giving a minisermon on creativity. For Francis, creativity was both a natural response to God's amazing grace and an opportunity to share that grace with others: "God has given me such a grace and blessing. . . . Therefore, for his glory, for my consolation, and the edification of my neighbor, I wish to compose a new 'Praises of the Lord,' for his creatures. . . . Every day we fail to appreciate so great a blessing by not praising as we should the Creator and dispenser of all these gifts."

Francis's approach toward linking our creativity to the Creator has been a powerful inspiration to believers throughout the ages. My own recording label is called Troubadour for the Lord in recognition of the way this sensitive saint joined our humble creative efforts to the powerful spiritual forces behind the creating and sustaining of life.

We live at a time when man believes himself fabulously capable of creation but he does not know what to create.—JOSÉ ORTEGA Y GASSET

Every creative medium can be used for good or for ill. I can use my telephone to call you and give you a warm message of encouragement. Or I could phone you and yell obscenities in your ear. Likewise, our God-given creativity can be used for positive ends or for negative ends.

One day Francis was staying in the town of Rieti. As was often the case, some of those around Francis at the time were musicians and artists. Suffering from a variety of physical ailments, the saint asked a brother who had worked as a musician before joining the Franciscan movement to play his zither to ease his pain. The saint also talked to the brother about an issue that was on his heart, saying: "Brother, the children of this world have no understanding of the things of God. Formerly, the saints used such musical instruments as the zither, psalteries, and others to praise God and console their soul; now these instruments promote vanity and sin, contrary to the will of the Lord."

We can see the truth of these words today. I'm continually amazed at how little true goodness there is in the music and entertainment of our modern world. Our stereos, radios, and televisions seem to play constantly. Mass-produced entertainment is everywhere: in our homes, our cars, our offices, and even our public elevators and restrooms. But with so much mass-produced culture surrounding us, doesn't it seem strange that there is so little of it that offers anything of true and lasting beauty? We're engulfed by a nonstop barrage of technically proficient, well-produced, and expertly marketed entertainment, but so little of it uplifts our soul. In fact, much of popular culture glorifies banality, ugliness, and violence. What a mess we have made of this beautiful gift of God, which was designed to heal and bless us.

During Lent, Francis would spend hours in prayer to God. One time, he crafted a small vase. Later, while meditating, he found himself focusing on the vase instead of God. Francis wouldn't stand for the interference any longer, and threw the vase into the fireplace, where it burst into pieces and burned. "Alas, what a worthless work that has such power over me," he said. "Let us be ashamed to be caught up by worthless imaginings."

Did you ever observe to whom the accidents happen? Chance favors only the prepared mind.
—LOUIS PASTEUR

Some people see creativity as the result of a sudden and irresistible burst of inspiration. The sculptor Michelangelo described the process of creation in such a way. He said God had put an image into the stone and the sculptor's job was to uncover it. But, unlike Michelangelo, I could chip away on a block of marble for years without creating beautiful works. That's because creativity is more than mere inspiration. It's also often a result of hard work and discipline.

Others see creativity as the end product of some kind of divine miraculous intervention. Miracles *do* happen, but often after preparation. Jesus turned water into wine at the wedding in Cana, but hardworking servants had to carry the large, heavy jugs of water that made the miracle possible.

My musical life started out with a difficult daily routine of practicing scales and chords. Only after painstakingly learning the basics could I begin to make sounds that actually resembled music. And during my teen years, when I first attempted to write songs, my older brother Terry was looking over my shoulder, telling me how awful they were and tearing them apart before my very eyes. I survived all these ordeals, but the hard work of creativity remains an essential part of my daily life.

How about you? How are you exercising your God-given creativity? What are you doing to take the raw materials of the world and reassemble them into a glorious new ensemble?

Or are you like many people who aren't really using their creative faculties? Perhaps you spend all your spare time watching television, listening to music on your CD player, or viewing movies on your VCR. True, consuming the artistic work of others does reflect the fact that God created us as creative beings, but it can also be an easy way of avoiding creating anything yourself.

Maybe you tried being creative once, but something went wrong. Perhaps your cranky old piano teacher rapped you on the knuckles one too many times. Or maybe your junior high art teacher laughed at your handmade masterpiece, making you angry and wounding your sensitive soul. Or maybe you grew up around a more creative older brother or sister who received all the attention and applause.

There are plenty of reasons why many of us are creatively blocked. But the sad thing is that too many of us fail to realize our God-given potential. We were created to create. Here are some ideas that may help you get unblocked and find new ways to beautify the world around you.

> *A Christian, above all people, should live artistically, aesthetically, and creatively. If we have been created in the image of an Artist, then we should look for expressions of artistry, and be sensitive to beauty, responsive to what has been created for our appreciation.*
> —EDITH SCHAEFFER

Have you ever overheard someone singing in the shower? I have, and it was an odd experience. The soapy singer I remember wasn't going to win any Grammy Awards or be invited to share the stage with Luciano Pavarotti or Placido Domingo. Still, there was something strangely moving about it. He was boisterous, joyful, and happy, and listening to him made me happy, too.

Not all of us may be destined for recording careers, but we can all sing in the shower. And we can all find other ways to become a part of something I call everyday creativity.

Singing in the shower is a way of applying everyday creativity to an activity that many of us think of as being restricted to professional singers. But anyone can sing, whether it be in the shower, in the car, or around the house. Also, many people say the highlight of their week happens when they get together with other non-professionals to sing songs or to add their voices to a church choir.

Likewise, you may not be a painter on par with Picasso, but you can create a simple watercolor to hang on your refrigerator door and brighten up your kitchen. You can also add illustrations to notes you write to friends. And while you're at it, try to be conscious of writing more creatively when you send those notes and letters. Instead of writing, "I went to the store today," try saying, "I spent the day with Ralph Lauren and Procter & Gamble." Think of new ways to see things and say things. Add a little spice to even the most mundane forms of communication.

Singing in the shower, painting a watercolor, or writing a unique letter to a friend are ways of applying everyday creativity to fields like music, art, and literature. But there are zillions of other areas of life that offer just as many fruitful avenues for expressing the uniqueness of the way God made you.

Men are like trees; each one must put forth the leaf that is created in him.—HENRY WARD BEECHER

Have you ever tried gardening? Working with natural materials like soil, seeds, and water, you can create a glorious garden of God. And you don't have to live in a house in the country surrounded by acres of fertile land to be a gardener. Even if you inhabit a tiny apartment in the middle of a concrete jungle, you can grow beautiful living things inside your home or in a planter attached to your windowsill or stair railing.

And what about interior decorating? Without hiring a high-priced design firm, you can make your humble house a majestic masterpiece by adding creative touches such as bursts of color and items that reflect your unique personality and help you consider the beauty of the created world.

Since God created us to create, there are an infinite number of ways we can be creative. Try making a piece of art out of the way you arrange food on a plate instead of dishing it out like an angry soldier at an army mess hall. Or think about ways your wardrobe can be a reflection of your own sense of style instead of a walking ad for a New York designer. Or think of new ways to enjoy periods of rest and recreation. Instead of piling family members into the car and heading to the local movie multiplex, take a walk in a nearby park or play games together. Think of other ways you can creatively transform the world around you.

Begin by doing everything you can to surround yourself with beauty. Pick a few flowers and put them in a vase on your dining room table where you can see them and smell them. You can also excite your senses by turning off all the lights, lighting a few candles, burning a stick of incense, and playing a Gregorian chant CD. You may also want to make a point of visiting a local art museum, where you can soak in regular doses of beauty.

And one of the most Franciscan things you can do is apply your creative gifts to the way God is worshiped. If you're part of a local congregation, fill your sanctuary with flowers, candles, and bright banners. Help organize a drama honoring holidays like Easter or Christmas or a saint's feast day. Seek out members of the church or local community who can contribute their gifts in art, music, and dance to your worship. Make your church a place that honors the glory of the original Creator, and help make your worship services lively, exuberant celebrations of God's grandeur and grace.

As you're trying these activities, remember that you're not doing them to get applause from others. Your primary audiences are God and yourself. Don't worry about what others will say. Don't let criticism cripple you. And if you receive praise, receive it graciously and thank God for giving you the ability to produce something of beauty.

And as you're trying to develop your own, innate creative urges, you may feel the need to decrease your consumption of mass-produced entertainment. Turn off the television and turn on your own inner artist. It's fine to enjoy the work of others, and sometimes this can be a source of inspiration and encouragement. But it can also make us into cultural couch potatoes who take in the efforts of others but don't create anything ourselves. Begin to be an intentional creator.

Try some of these suggestions, or come up with some ideas of your own. You may be surprised to find that such creativity can be extremely contagious, particularly with children. Help teach your children or young people you know how to create things. By doing so you may be helping them spend the rest of their lives producing things of beauty instead of merely consuming the creative commodities of others.

Make pomegranates of blue, purple and scarlet yarn around the hem of the robe, with gold bells between them.—THE BOOK OF EXODUS

In the passage, God is instructing Israel's crafts people in the proper construction and design of the Tabernacle, where priests would make sacrifices, perform other rituals, and seek forgiveness for the sins of the people. It was a serious place where holy priests conducted important business, and God spelled out minutely detailed instructions about how everything was to be laid out. God even told the crafts people how to create the priests' robes: "There shall be a woven edge like a collar. . . . Make pomegranates of blue, purple and scarlet yarn around the hem of the robe, with gold bells between them."

Have you ever seen a pomegranate? These fabulous, Technicolor fruits do exist, hidden away in the middle of a lengthy and somewhat dry passage of Exodus.

Think about these pomegranates the next time somebody says God's not into creativity. And look for ways you can bring God's rainbow of colors and creativity into your own life.

7
Chastity

❧❧❧

❧❧ *Clare was the first flower in Francis'
garden, and she shone like a radiant star,
fragrant as a flower blossoming white and
pure in springtime.*—St. Bonaventure

Take a walk in a garden and your senses will be
bombarded by sensual sights and luxuriant smells.
Depending on the climate and the proclivities of the gardener, you may enjoy fragrant and beautiful roses or see
invincible, prickly cacti.

If you're in London, you'll see gardens that are
immaculate and well kept, a reflection of the British
belief that gardens are showpieces which reflect the character of their owners. In Japan and China, gardens are
known for their distinctive minimalist simplicity. Our
combination vegetable and prayer gardens at Little Portion are a bit wilder, featuring a variety of flowers and
plants that thrive in our humid weather and fertile soil.

But look around in God's human garden, and you'll
see even more dazzling, dizzying variety than you see in
the plant world. Some people are like roses, wearing
brightly colored clothing and sporting fragrant perfume.

Others are more subdued, like the members of our community, who wear brown, unisex robes that conceal a lot more than they reveal.

There are a near-infinite number of ways that we can express our unique personalities and attractiveness. I believe Francis has some profound insights into this complex area, and you don't even have to wear a brown robe to benefit from what he had to say.

> *Lust is the craving for salt of a man who is dying of thirst.*—FREDERICK BUECHNER

Religion and sex make strange bedfellows.

Most often, the two are publicly linked when a crusading preacher launches a tirade protesting the intolerable offenses against God, country, and family found in the latest raunchy rock record or titillating TV show. Or when a conservative activist campaigns about numerous "below-the-belt" issues like abortion, sex education, or homosexuality. Or when an investigative journalist exposes hypocrisy in holy places, showing a high-flying televangelist brought low by a seedy seductress or a once-Puritanical preacher found to be frolicking with a member of his flock. Such episodes make it a daunting task to discuss morality, particularly in an age of post–sexual revolution permissiveness and postmodern skepticism about moral absolutes.

On the other hand, I'm finding that many people are sincerely seeking to regain a sense of lost sexual sanity. They're hungry for a sense of sexual wholeness that distinguishes between love and lust. They worry about a lack of innocence that sours many young people (and even some adults). They watch in horror as marriages and other relationships flounder, the victims of weak commitments and broken covenants. And they're concerned about the breakdown of morality they see around them.

Do monks and mystics have something to say to us in the midst of this confusion and turmoil? Many people think so. Kathleen Norris, author of the bestselling book *The Cloister Walk*, contrasts the over-the-top sensuality of contemporary Western society with the sanctity and sanity she found among a group of celibate Benedictine monks with whom she spent much of two years. "Celibate people have taught me that celibacy, practiced rightly, does indeed have something valuable to say to the rest of us," she writes. "Specifically, they have helped me better appreciate both the nature of friendship and what it means to be married."

For centuries, people following the Franciscan way have committed themselves to three vows: poverty, obedience, and chastity. And chastity, which means making an effort to order our sexual lives around a higher moral purpose, is one of the covenant promises of our Brothers and Sisters of Charity at Little Portion.

I know that chastity has some severe public relations problems in today's world. And many people mistakenly think of monastics as people who are either asexual, sexually repressed, or sexually perverted. After all, why would someone voluntarily place any restrictions on something that's so powerful and passionate? Ironically, it's the power and passion of sex that require us to channel and cultivate it. Like a garden that quickly grows out of control without constant tending, sexuality needs loving care and direction.

The Franciscan tradition contains a wealth of wisdom about how we can turn down the erotically charged voices of our culture and craft a sexual ethic that combines a reverence for God, a respect for our partner, and a realism about the potential dangers of unrestrained sensuality.

Blessed are the pure in heart, for they will see God.
—JESUS

The right mushroom can taste great on a steak, while the wrong mushroom can kill you. Fire can warm a home or burn it to the ground. Electricity can light up a room or give you a life-threatening shock. Likewise, sex can be a source of joy or sorrow, pleasure or pain, deep intimacy or desperate loneliness, gentleness and vulnerability or violence and self-protection.

For me as for many others, our own personal histories reveal how sex can heal us or hurt us, make us whole or devastate our psyches. I've personally lived through at least three completely different approaches to sex: the freewheeling sensuality readily available to a rock musician; the cleansing fire and spiritual passion of repentance and sexual abstinence; and the rejuvenating joy of marriage, a union through which the church has long honored sex as a sacrament, and which helps me see sexuality as sacred and God-given.

If there's anything I've found, it's that the secret of

living out a vibrant, healthy, and spiritually directed sexuality involves three things: realizing that there are many choices available to us; choosing to make the choices that are best for our age and state in life; and doing whatever it takes to ensure that we are faithful to those choices.

Monks and mystics are especially concerned about the ways that sex potentially distracts them from the work of worshiping God. Some of them try to turn their backs on sex altogether. But you might be surprised to find how many monastics incorporate a balanced approach to sexuality in their spiritual lives.

Since God created humanity as male and female, many monks have argued that a healthy spirituality must include a balance of feminine and masculine elements. Many Celtic monasteries were "double" facilities, with separate quarters for men and women monks. Some communities even practiced a form of monastic marriage alongside celibacy.

But among the various orders and traditions in the church, few have exhibited as much of an appreciation for the interplay of masculine and feminine spirituality as the Franciscan tradition. In part, that's because of the special relationship Francis had with Clare, a beautiful and privileged young woman who "eloped" from her family at age eighteen to become the first female member of Francis's movement.

> *She followed him because she loved the treasure. She heard him speak of what he had found, and a passage in her own heart opened up.*—FATHER MURRAY BODO

It's been said that Francis loved five women. One was Lady Poverty. One was the Virgin Mary. One was his mother, Lady Pica, a sensitive and spiritual woman who encouraged him to follow God. One was Lady Jacoba di Settesoli, a devout widow whom Francis affectionately called "Brother Jacoba." And the other was Clare.

The story of Francis and Clare is a love story of cinematic proportions. As writer Bruce Bawer put it, "The introduction into [Francis's] life of a young woman named Clare seems almost like a plot device out of some old movie—a medieval version, say, of *The Bells of St. Mary's.* "

Although there's not much biographical information about Francis and Clare, their relationship has inspired writers, dramatists, and lovers for centuries, some of whom have inserted their own fanciful fictions into the gaps in the historical record. For example, Greek writer Nikos Kazantzakis, whose *The Last Temptation of Christ* pictured Jesus daydreaming about climbing down off the cross and getting married, wrote the controversial novel *Saint Francis*, which portrays Francis as sexually obsessed with Clare, tormented by temptation and sweating with lust.

The truth is probably much less soap-operaish, but infinitely more mysterious and moving. Twentieth-century Franciscan Murray Bodo was rapturous: "So great was their love for God that even now, seven and a half centuries later, it makes Assisi good in spring and summer, fall and winter." An earlier writer, Auspicius van Corstanje, was no less excited: "They discovered in each other the same luxury of God's presence and the same fire that consumed all the idols in their hearts, until they were ash." One thing is clear: Francis and Clare demolished the myth that loving God and loving another are mutually exclusive. The better we understand how they lived and loved, the better we can apply the spiritual principles they practiced to our own sexuality.

The basic outline of Clare's life is well known. Although she was twelve years younger than Francis, she was familiar with his life in Assisi, first as a young, flashy troubadour, and then as a poor, humble follower of Jesus. She clearly saw the severe changes in Francis's life, but unlike others in Assisi, she didn't conclude he had lost his mind. Instead, she knew he had found it.

Whenever the scruffy Francis preached in Assisi's beautiful church, Clare heard his simple sermons and found her heart strangely warmed. An attractive young woman, Clare graciously declined all of the proposals she received from qualified suitors. Instead, she ran away from her family on the Palm Sunday after her eighteenth birthday, becoming the first of many women to join Francis's movement.

In a secret nighttime ceremony, Francis, surrounded by his brothers, cut Clare's beautiful hair, gave her a humble robe and rope belt, and welcomed her to his way of life. Clare never lived with the brothers, staying instead in a nearby Benedictine convent before winding up at San Damiano, the small chapel where Francis had heard Jesus speak to him from a crucifix. He had rebuilt this once-rundown building with his own hands.

Initially, Clare's actions caused a stir in the town and enraged her father. But over time, the order that she founded, the Poor Clares, attracted many other women, including Clare's mother and two of her sisters. Today, the order has more than seventeen thousand sisters living lives of solitude and contemplation.

> *Entering the place, they found St. Francis with St. Clare and all the companions sitting around that very humble table, rapt in God by contemplation and invested with power from on high.*
> —THE LITTLE FLOWERS OF ST. FRANCIS

Francis and Clare were not some religious Romeo and Juliet. What drew them to each other was not romance or physical attraction. Francis and Clare were magnetically drawn to each other by their powerful and passionate love of God, as their lives showed.

Because he wanted to make sure his affection for Clare did not replace his love for God in his heart, Francis only visited his beloved sister a few times during his life. But when they did meet, it was a beautiful thing. Once, after numerous requests from Clare, Francis agreed to meet her for a meal, accompanied, as usual, by various brothers and sisters. The fifteenth chapter of *The Little Flowers of St. Francis* is mundanely titled "How St. Clare Ate a Meal with St. Francis and His Friars." But the chapter's contents are far from ordinary.

A simple meal was prepared and laid out on a plain table on the bare ground. As everyone sat down to eat, Francis "began to speak about God in such a sweet and holy and profound and divine and marvelous way" that all lost interest in their food and were feasting on the presence of God in their midst. During their contemplation, God became: "The whole Place and the forest which at that time was around the Place were all aflame and . . . an immense fire was burning over all of them."

According to the authors of *The Little Flowers*, this was no mere hallucination. In fact, men from Assisi rushed to the site to put out the fire. But there would be no quenching these flames, as the astounded townspeople could see: "They saw that nothing was on fire. Entering the Place, they found St. Francis with St. Clare and all the companions sitting around that very humble table, rapt in God by contemplation and invested with power from on high. Then they knew for sure that it had been a heavenly and not a material fire that God had miraculously shown them to symbolize the fire of divine love which was burning in the souls of those holy friars and nuns."

This kind of mystical fire wasn't unique to Francis and Clare. Other saints have enjoyed both the love for God and the affection for a special friend, such as Teresa of Ávila and John of the Cross, or Hilda of Whitby and Aidan of Iona.

And it's not just saints who can experience this wondrous mixture of divine and human love. God wants all of us to know both levels of affection. Digging into the wealth of riches found in the monastic tradition can help us recognize it.

Not everyone can accept this word, but only those to whom it has been given. For some are eunuchs because they were born that way; others were made that way by men; and others have renounced marriage because of the kingdom of heaven. The one who can accept this should accept it.—JESUS

Celibacy, which is the renunciation of sex and marriage for the service of God, may seem like a lifestyle that's fine for monks but of little value for others. Admittedly it isn't for everyone, and is considered the special gift for a relative few. But still, there's a wisdom to renunciation which can benefit everyone.

For Francis, celibacy was the only choice. He wanted to be like Jesus, and Jesus had never married. And Jesus had taught there would be no marriage in heaven, indicating that marriage bonds are temporary, not eternal. Francis wanted to focus all his emotional energy on developing an intimacy with God that would grow deeper through time and eternity. These things don't make celibacy superior to other lifestyles, but in a sense they do make it more "Christ-like." And it's not just Christianity which teaches that the celibate life is the best life for some.

Part of the reason celibacy has a place in so many diverse religions is that choosing not to be married gives people a unique freedom to choose many other things, such as a life of undisturbed solitude or prayer, or a life of tireless service to others in need, or an itinerant life of preaching and pastoring, much like St. Paul lived in the earliest years of the Christian church.

Having experienced both the celibate and married states myself, I know that celibacy gives one a spiritual focus, a carefree abandon, and a physical mobility that provide the opportunity to focus solely on God and his work. Also, not being emotionally committed to a partner allows you to be warm, committed, and loving to many people, as the lives of monastics like Mother Teresa have shown.

Although celibacy is not for everyone, I sometimes wonder if some for whom it would work simply don't have their antennae up to catch the message. Or perhaps the message is being drowned out by the omnipresent sexuality of our time. But even if like most people you know the celibate life isn't for you, there's much we can learn from our monastic brothers and sisters who struggle to master their sexual drives and appetites. If nothing else, celibacy is an excellent preparation for marriage. Think of it this way: No sex is a prelude to good sex, or godly sex!

Part of why so many people don't remain sexually faithful to their marriage partners is because they never learned the valuable art of sexual control. It's an art monks and mystics have mastered, and they can teach us much.

> *You have heard that it was said, "Do not commit adultery." But I tell you that anyone who looks at a woman lustfully has already committed adultery with her in his heart.*—JESUS

During the 1960s and 1970s, many young people became Christians through the Jesus movement. Some of these spiritual seekers had previously lived in communes where experimentation with "liberated" sexual lifestyles was common. After their conversion, some of these young believers established Christian communes. Only very few of these communities have survived until now, and unfortunately that's due in part to the fact that some misguided community leaders couldn't restrain their sexual appetites and treated members of their communities as part of some private harem.

Even in the Middle Ages there were those who blurred the line between responsible and irresponsible sexuality. Francis's response may seem extreme by today's standard, but it worked to keep his embryonic communities free of scandal.

The rules regarding sex in Franciscan communities are strict and clear, and they're based on Francis's insight into the sexual weaknesses to which we all may fall prey. In short, his approach is based on the realization that we can never be too sure of our own abilities to resist sexual temptation. He believed it was better to avoid the occasions of sin than to expect delivery at the moment of temptation.

"No matter where they are or where they go, the friars are bound to avoid the sight or company of women, when it is evil," he wrote in his Rule of 1221. "No one should speak to them alone." Elsewhere, he wrote: "I strictly forbid all the friars to have suspicious relationships or conversations with women." Although some have interpreted these comments as evidence that Francis harbored some thinly veiled distaste for women, his words really say more about the sexual weakness of men, a subject that monks of all faiths have acknowledged for centuries.

As for himself, Francis studiously avoided winding up in potentially compromising situations with women, including with his beloved Clare, whom he seldom saw after the Poor Clares were founded and housed at San Damiano. He never met with women alone. And when conversing with them in public, he averted his glance from their eyes, telling one of the friars that he didn't have any idea what the women he talked to actually looked like.

When one of the brothers asked Francis why he didn't look into women's eyes, particularly those women who were leading devout and holy lives, his response showed his distaste for easy intimacy and his respect for women's inner beauty: "Who must not fear to look upon the bride of Christ?"

Francis wasn't a crazed zealot. When a brother was tempted and failed, he could be forgiven. But Francis gave no quarter to friars who repeatedly fell into sexual sin. They were dismissed from the order.

In some ways, Francis was the product of the Middle Ages, a time during which a majority of the church's male leaders subscribed to a horribly flawed understanding of theology that viewed women as one of the primary sources of temptation in the world. But we shouldn't write him off or dismiss him. He rose above the narrow confines of his time, and his teaching shows us how to bring sexuality under the guidance of our spiritual ideals and the control of our wills. Whether the inspiration of Francis is used to guide the corporate life of communities like the Brothers and Sisters of Charity at Little Portion or individual lives like yours, his insight is valuable in any age.

Marriage is a unique relationship that places special demands on us. To maintain a healthy marriage, a couple must adhere to certain biblical imperatives, including sexual fidelity, sacrificial love, mutual respect and lifelong commitment.—HAROLD B. SMITH

Covenants, or binding voluntary agreements, are a big part of how God has dealt with humanity through the ages. In the era before Christ, God entered into a covenant with the people of Israel, declaring that he would be their God and they would be his people. Centuries later, Jesus entered into a covenant with the world after his death and resurrection, saying, "Surely, I am with you always, to the very end of the age."

Many people don't realize it, but marriage is a unique and important human covenant through which the life of one person is bound to the life of another. Although the marriage covenant is on a smaller scale than God's universal covenant with humanity, the marriage covenant is no less important. Christian tradition views marriage as a partnership that is lifelong, exclusive, and focused on the mutual well-being of husband and wife, which in turn extends to their children.

Marriage is not more godly than singleness or celibacy, even though some contemporary "family values" crusaders seem to claim it is, threatening in the process to turn the nuclear family into some kind of new Golden Calf. But God does care greatly about marriage, which in some ways is a reflection of the theological mystery that God is a partnership between three distinct personalities, which are known as the Trinity.

I went through a period of trying to weigh whether to marry or remain celibate. In the meantime, a beautiful sister named Viola came into my life. Over a period of time, she entered into a place deep within my soul that had previously been reserved for God alone. Both she and I saw that we could love God and each other at the same time, while helping each other deepen our mutual love for God.

During the eight years we have been married, Viola has brought much happiness and peace to my life. The people who live at Little Portion—including celibates and marrieds—know she has brought a balance to our community, much as I suspect Clare infused the Franciscan movement with her uniquely feminine spirituality.

I'm not sure what kind of relationship Viola and I will have in heaven. But I'm glad that God has allowed us to share at least part of our earthly lives together and to help each other serve God and others in our individual ways.

A heavenly love can be as real as an earthly love.
—G. K. CHESTERTON

God is love, and part of being created in God's image means knowing love. We are designed to love, and will be unhappy and unsatisfied until we know love deep within our hearts.

Too often, human love is only a frail and flawed image of the infinite and luxuriant love of God. But regardless of whether you're married or single, you can know what it means to be spiritually united to God.

Spiritual marriage, in which we relate to God as the lover of our soul, has been the foundation of Christian mysticism for centuries. Francis knew this kind of intimacy with God, although he wrote little about it. Other saints, like Teresa of Ávila and John of the Cross, wrote extensive journals about their communion with God, and they also wrote books designed to guide others along the path of opening their hearts to God. Today, many modern mystics know through firsthand experience that the love of God is more than a mere doctrine or concept. It's a daily reality.

You may be happily married or happily single. You may have been divorced or widowed. No matter what romantic state you're in, God loves you and wants you to come near. Experiencing the love of God will fill your heart to overflowing.

> *You would think, wouldn't you, that a faith founded on the premise of incarnation—of the Word-that-speaks-all-into-being made flesh to dwell among us—would hold in certain respect, perhaps in outright reverence, the body, the very form in which the divine had elected to be housed.*—NANCY MAIRS

Moving into a monastery may not be on your agenda, and practicing celibacy may not be what you're cut out to do. But you can still apply the lessons of chastity to your life, no matter where you are or what your status. In the process, you may see that some of the ancient taboos aren't as arcane and archaic as they're made out to be, and that the rampant sexual promiscuity of the West can often be more enslaving than liberating.

Perhaps a good place to begin would be by making an honest assessment of your present sexual values. A recent survey of Americans' attitudes toward sex found that people basically fell into one of three common categories: traditional, relational, and recreational. The "traditional" view would probably be closest to the teachings of Francis and the ideals we've discussed in this chapter, including an emphasis on a lifelong commitment, exclusivity, and a focus on mutual respect and well-being. The "relational" view would see sex as part of a loving relationship, but not necessarily one that was exclusive, committed, or confined to marriage. The "recreational" view dispenses with factors like romance and spirituality, and sees sex primarily in terms of pleasure.

Here are some questions for you to consider as you try to figure out which category you're in: Why are those values your sexual values? Have you always felt that way or have you changed your views over time? Why? Is your current position a sound one that works? How does it work in your current relationship? Do you and your partner see eye-to-eye? How will your values serve you throughout your life?

It's possible that it may be time for you to trade in the set of sexual values that you've followed thus far for a better set. If so, or if you feel like you've been on a roller coaster of superficial and spiritually unsatisfying relationships, why not consider abstaining from sex for a while. Consider it a period of temporary celibacy and preparation for deeper, more committed loving. Maybe you'll realize that sex has been a poor substitute for other unmet emotional and spiritual needs in your life, and that by being less sexually active you can become more sexually whole.

Like nitroglycerin, [sex] can be used either to blow up bridges or heal hearts.—FREDERICK BUECHNER

Francis displayed an amazing balance when it came to sexuality. On the one hand, he respected its beauty and power. On the other hand, he wasn't naive about his own—or anybody else's—ability to let his spiritual values guide sexual behavior.

Among Francis's main lessons for me are these:

✤ Cherish your sexuality, and be aware of how important it is in your personality and your life.

✤ Receive your sexuality as a God-given gift. Don't overvalue or undervalue it. Don't be afraid of it or addicted to it.

✤ Allow sex to help you in your relationship with God and others, building love and intimacy rather than causing tension and jealousy.

✤ Use sex in an appropriate way, in a holy way, in a way that respects God and others.

✤ Don't be too conceited about your ability to resist whatever temptations come your way. Set sane limits for yourself and live within them. And define limits for you and your partner that you can both agree on and that increase your level of trust and intimacy with each other.

✤ Don't turn your back on time-tested truths. Principles developed by Francis centuries ago may be better for us than ideas hatched by magazine publishers and advertising executives in the last half of the twentieth century.

Finally, think of sex as a means of communication, not primarily as a means of experiencing pleasure. Look at it as a way to give pleasure to your partner instead of taking pleasure for yourself. This is how sex begins to be more like divine love. As we grow in sexual wholeness, our sexuality can be united with our spirituality, giving us a hint of what ultimate spiritual union is like.

8

Community

❧ *I wish that my brothers would show themselves to be children of the same mother.*

—Francis

J OHN WAYNE WOULD NEVER HAVE MADE it as a monk.
For decades "The Duke" was Hollywood's pre-eminent embodiment of the strong, silent type. Whether playing a cowboy, a soldier, or another masculine hero, he was always happiest to go it alone. And although he loved a variety of women, none could keep him home for long. Sooner or later, he would be twirling his Winchester, sitting high in his saddle, and riding off into the sunset on his trusty steed, solitary and self-contained.

Our long-running love affair with Wayne reveals more than mere affection for a popular actor. It also symbolizes our romance with rugged individualism. Independence, personal autonomy, and a don't-tread-on-me swagger are basic building blocks of the modern mind-set.

But look around and you can see growing evidence that this contemporary psyche needs therapy. Untrammeled individualism is wrecking families and destroying our communities. Throughout the West, civilizations are witnessing a revival of tribalism, with people sharply divided along racial, ethnic, cultural, religious, demographic, and economic lines.

Our present disunity would have come as a surprise to utopian dreamers who predicted that the human race would enter a new Golden Age as it moved from village to town, to city, to metropolis, to megalopolis. But ironically, the larger our cities have grown, the more lonely and the less interconnected many of us feel.

More than a decade ago, my study of the life of Francis, my growing commitment to follow in the footsteps of Jesus, and my distaste for individualism led me to make a radical decision. I became part of a larger whole by forming a community of Christians committed to serving God and one another at close range.

In 1982, construction was begun on Little Portion, our creative Franciscan community near Eureka Springs, Arkansas. Since then, we have blossomed into a new, integrated community called the Brothers and Sisters of Charity, where I have lived with a group of believers ever since.

Our community is far from perfect. In fact, there are times when living with others in community shines a powerful light on my own self-centeredness and selfishness. But my experience at Little Portion has deepened my commitment to community. And I believe that some of the lessons we have learned here could help you achieve a sense of community in your own life.

In a real sense all life is interrelated. All [people] are caught in an inescapable network of mutuality, tied in a single garment of destiny.
— MARTIN LUTHER KING JR.

In the twentieth century, the Christian religion has been redesigned to accommodate the radical individualism of the West. But we should never forget that Christianity began as a communal faith. Just look at the New Testament's description of the first followers of Jesus: "All the believers were together and had everything in common. Selling their possessions and goods, they gave to anyone as he had need. . . . And the Lord added to their number daily those who were being saved."

As the Christian movement grew and matured, and its message spread around the world, this communal dimension waned. Ironically, it was St. Anthony of Egypt, a solitary hermit who fled to the desert to be alone with God in the late third century, who helped revive Christian communalism. People became attracted to the deeply spiritual saint, followed him to his cave in the desert, and formed a community dedicated to spiritual growth and mutual support—creating one of the earliest Christian monasteries.

Christian monasticism became even more popular in the fourth century, after the Roman Empire declared Christianity its official religion. Many believers felt that giving Christianity official status only watered down the faith, so they created communities where they could live out the teachings of Jesus in a purer form.

Twentieth-century monk Thomas Merton described

the magnetic allure monasticism held for these early Christian communitarians in his book *Wisdom from the Desert*: "Society—which meant pagan society, limited by the horizons and prospects of life 'in this world'—was regarded by them as a shipwreck from which each single individual man had to swim for his life."

A dizzying variety of Christian communities flourished around the world as spiritually inclined individuals sought havens for holy living. Then, early in the sixth century, St. Benedict of Nursia developed a popular and practical model for monastic living, earning him the title "the father of Western monasticism." The Benedictine rule, which influenced many monasteries for centuries, stressed prayer, discipline, and labor. During the Middle Ages, monasteries provided an island of silence, solitude, study, and spiritual growth in the midst of an often turbulent world. And they continue to do so today.

In community, people such as myself burrow deep in the fertile soil of fraternity, which allows us to uncover our deep selves and strengthen our faith. Or as Jean Vanier, a twentieth-century Frenchman who has founded more than one hundred L'Arche communities for the physically and mentally handicapped, puts it: "Community is a place of belonging, a place where people are earthed and find their identity."

For ages, the message of the monasteries has been that Christianity isn't a solo performance. Instead, each of us is part of an amazing choir, and the mystical music we make together is a beautiful creation, both to us and to God. For me and many others, living in Christian community gives us a chance to join our voices in a universal chorus of brotherhood.

The friars are bound to love one another because our Lord says, "This is my commandment, that you love one another as I have loved you."—FRANCIS

Like Anthony of Egypt, Francis was a solitary and penitential hermit who became the founder of a movement only after other people were attracted to his radical lifestyle. Francis wrote a series of Rules designed to govern the life of the Franciscan communities. Perhaps not surprisingly, the Rules were brief and deeply spiritual, and they emphasized applying the principles of Jesus to daily life in practical ways.

Like Jesus, Francis put top priority on love, which meant that Franciscan communities were fraternities of fellowship, brotherliness, and mutual support. One early Franciscan described the first Franciscans, saying: "How great was the love that flourished in the members of this pious society! For whenever they came together anywhere, or met one another along the way, there a shoot of spiritual love sprang up, sprinkling over all the seed of true affection."

Further on, this friar explained that the love that Francis's followers sought was more than mere sentimentality: "Indeed, since they despised all earthly things and did not love themselves with a selfish love, pouring out their whole affection on all the brothers, they strove to give themselves as the price of helping one another in their needs." Or as yet another early Franciscan brother described it: "Each was ready to give his life for the other. This and similar things were possible because they were so deeply rooted in mutual love."

This love, mutual respect, and selfless service was

founded on Francis's radical egalitarianism. "He wanted the greater to be joined to the lesser, the wise to be united with the simple by brotherly affection," wrote one brother.

Francis did his best to institutionalize this spiritual equality. Instead of calling his friars monks, Francis called them brothers. While he was at it, Francis even did away with the term "prior," which was commonly used in other communities, and which suggested that the monk who held this title was "the first" or had the highest place of honor. Instead, the leaders or custodians of Franciscan communities were called ministers. And in an unprecedented step, the friars could depose ministers general with the approval of church authorities. This was a truly revolutionary approach at a time when many monasteries simply reflected the rigidly stratified class structure of European society.

Francis also believed that all people should be able to enjoy some form of Christian community. That's why he helped start two other orders in addition to his Order of Friars Minor. As we have seen, the Poor Clares, founded in 1212 by Clare of Assisi, was a female version of the Friars Minor, with one major difference. In addition to the three vows of poverty, chastity, and obedience, the Poor Clares take an additional vow of enclosure. Creation of this order allowed women to follow Francis's vision.

In 1221, Francis founded the Brothers and Sisters of Penance, later known as the Third Order Regular of St. Francis, or the Secular Franciscans. This unique order was created for men and women who wanted to live a more active life outside the walls of a monastery or friary, either in their communities or their own homes. Or as

Father Alan Woltar put it, "The cloister went out to the world and the world returned to the cloister." The poet Dante and the composer Franz Liszt are among some of the better known Secular Francisans.

The Brothers and Sisters of Charity take the flexibility of the Secular Franciscans one step further. Our community integrates celibate brothers, celibate sisters, and families, respecting the uniqueness of each. We also have a "domestic expression" for people who live in their own homes. It's an approach I believe Francis would embrace were he alive today.

No matter what type of community arrangement they adopt, followers of Francis put a priority on finding practical ways to live out both their commitment to Christ and their love for others. In our age of rampant individualism, fractured communities, and broken commitments, such love is a precious and valuable thing.

Let the tongue that poured out the poison of anger upon my brother eat dung.—FRANCIS

The one thing that could easily put the usually sanguine saint into a righteous rage was when he heard one of his brothers saying something nasty about another. Francis tried to avoid getting within earshot of gossipers, whom he called "biting fleas" and whom he said practiced "the vice of detraction." "Disaster confronts the order unless these slanderers are checked," he said once. "Quickly the sweetest savor of the many begins to take on a horrible stench, unless the mouths of the stinking are closed."

Another time, Francis condemned those who spread

discord. "The detractor feeds on the souls which he kills with his tongue. A detractor is guilty of greater wickedness than a robber, because Christ's law which reaches its perfection in love obliges us to desire the good of our neighbor's soul more than of his body." Anger and accusations gave the Devil a foothold in the community, said Francis, allowing the evil one freedom to work in their midst.

Why was the gentle Francis so rough on trash talkers? It's because he had a deep respect for the power of the tongue and the vulnerability of the soul. He didn't want his brothers, who were focusing on opening their hearts to God and humanity, to be forced to close their hearts to protect themselves from the assaults of their brothers.

Francis knew the tongue was capable of great evil, as did the writer of the New Testament book of James: "Consider what a great forest is set on fire by a small spark. The tongue also is a fire, a world of evil among the parts of the body. It corrupts the whole person, sets the whole course of his life on fire, and is itself set on fire by hell."

One doesn't have to live in a friary, or even be a Christian, to see the wisdom of these words. Verbal attacks divide family members, pit worker against employer, cause unnecessary strife and tension in our cities, and help lead to foolish fights between nations of the world. Perhaps that's why Buddha included "right speech" in his "eightfold path," or why Taoism and Confucianism value silence and moderate speech, or why most of the world's faiths counsel us to watch our tongues.

"Far from doing or speaking evil to one another," said Francis, "the friars should be glad to serve and obey one

another in a spirit of charity. This is the true, holy obedience of our Lord Jesus Christ."

*From lofty principles of community we soon came down
to hassles over keeping the washing machine clean . . .
about a thousand petty things that irritated us and
brought us into a deeper awareness of sin than we had
ever known before.*—DAVID JANZEN

Martin Luther once described marriage as a school for
character. From my experience, living in community
provides graduate-level training in character building.

St. Benedict's monastic rule reflects this fact, reading:
"The Lord waits for us daily to translate into action, as
we should, his holy teachings. . . . Therefore, we intend
to establish a school for the Lord's service. In drawing
up its regulations, we hope to set down nothing harsh,
nothing burdensome. The good of all concerned, however, may prompt us to a little strictness in order to
amend faults and to safeguard love."

Surprisingly, at Little Portion and at other communities, it's the little things that challenge our resolve, not
the big issues. Communities don't fall apart because
people fail to buy into a common vision. Instead, tensions come from seemingly insignificant conflicts that
test our resolve.

Everyone who comes to our hermitage has rejected
consumerism for the Gospel values of poverty and simplicity. They've turned their backs on sexual promiscuity
to observe chastity or celibacy. They've traded in their
individualism for humility and obedience. That's the
easy part.

The big challenges here are when someone else is doing his laundry on your designated laundry day. Or when the brother who had kitchen duty didn't show up. Or when we're working in our garden, trying with all our might to grow a green bean for God.

The big things are tested in the little things. Or as Jesus said, those who are faithful in little things, will be entrusted with big things.

Maybe you're wondering why anyone would voluntarily subject herself to such abuse. People might ask similar questions of someone beginning the grueling process known as medical school. Why spend all that money, go through all that training, and spend all those long hours doing an internship?

People join communities and attend med school for the same reasons. They're committed to learning something that can only be gained by the right kind of training. That applies to medical specialties like surgery as well as to spiritual values like poverty and humility.

Many people say they accept Francis's principles on poverty. But in community, we put these principles into practice. No one at Little Portion Hermitage owns the bed he sleeps on, the roof over her head, or the clothes he wears. Everything is owned by the community. And usually, those of us here think we have learned the lesson that nothing is really ours. But we are tested when the bed we think of as "my" bed is given to a sick brother who needs rest.

Likewise, I might believe I practice humility. But living in community gives me endless opportunities to see my own willful spirit exposed. My fellow brothers and sisters are my teachers, who point out problems in my life to me and hold my accountable to do something about them. This kind of accountability is something that's rarely possible outside a tight-knit Christian community.

Living in community also teaches us that no matter how different people are, they can still get along together if they want to and are willing to do the community-building work that's required and are committed to sticking to the process for the long haul.

In short, I believe that God wants to fill us from the inside with a rich diet of healthy spiritual food. Most of us, though, content ourselves with junk food. Impatient about the slow pace of real, inner growth and frustrated by the hard work involved in submitting to God, we opt for something quicker and easier. But in community, the purpose and the pace of life is geared toward one thing: our members' growth.

For where two or three come together in my name, there am I with them.—JESUS

Living in community isn't all hard work and self-denial. One of the most satisfying practical benefits of living together with other believers is that they are there for support when you need it. If we stumble or fall, someone is there on either side to gently pick us up and help us on our way. They don't drag us up, or yank our arms violently. But they help us with love and gentleness. That's the beauty of following God together and the strength of community.

The idea that two are stronger than one is commonsensical. It also is part of the ancient Jewish tradition, as this passage by Solomon suggests:

> Two are better than one . . .
> If one falls down, his friend can help him up.
> But pity the man who falls and has no one to
>   help him up!
> Also, if two lie down together they will keep
>   warm.
> But how can one keep warm alone?
> Though one may be overpowered, two can
>   defend themselves.
> A cord of three strands is not quickly broken.

In addition to all the practical benefits that come from being part of a larger communal whole, there are spiritual benefits as well, for community is mystical. Jesus' promise that he would be in our midst when we gather in his name is more than some kind of magical mumbo jumbo. It's something we've experienced here at Little Portion Hermitage hundreds of times as we've worshiped together with our brothers and sisters. It's not some form of mass hallucination or group-think, but an unmistakable mystical union with each other and with God during which we sense the presence of Jesus.

The Little Flowers of St. Francis records that many such experiences occurred when Francis and his brothers gathered. And the New Testament describes the unique way Jesus makes himself known to Christians in community.

Spirituality isn't supposed to be solitary. And loving God isn't a Lone Ranger–type experience. We were created to enjoy worship both vertically (between ourselves and God) and horizontally (between ourselves and other believers). And community helps us do this in a remarkable and very real way.

> *No man is an island, entire of itself; every man is a piece of the continent, a part of the main.*
> —JOHN DONNE

Another unique aspect of the way Franciscans do community is their balance between being inner-directed and outer-directed. We inherit this balance directly from Francis, who would spend weeks alone in his hermitage before traveling for weeks on the highways and byways tirelessly preaching the message of Jesus to anyone who would hear him.

Francis was a mystic, but not a full-time hermit. For him, God was not some kind of prized possession that was to be hoarded and kept from everyone else. Instead, Francis saw the grace of God as a beautiful, precious gift that God intended to be shared with the whole world. Francis loved and honored that gift during his private moments, and he shouted it from the rooftops during his more public ones.

The twentieth-century monk Thomas Merton was not a Franciscan. He was part of the Cistercian Order of the Strict Observance, also known as the Trappists, which is one of the most contemplative orders. But Merton admired the way Franciscans balanced their concern for the inner and outer lives. Writing about the typical Franciscan hermitage, he remarked: "It is a place of . . . temporary retreat to which one withdraws in order to renew the spirit of prayer and fervor and from which one returns to the work of preaching with a more perfect charity and a message of more convincing hope." Franciscan spirituality, said Merton, was characterized by a spirit that is "always open to the world."

Finally, Merton said a Franciscan hermitage was a place where followers of Jesus could be rejuvenated for further service in the world. Being in a Franciscan community, he said, leads to "the recovery of one's deep self, and to the renewal of an authenticity that is twisted out of shape by the pretentious routines of a disordered togetherness."

In striking this balance between the inner and outer lives, Francis found inspiration in Jesus, who spent time alone in prayer and meditation with God as well as out preaching to and teaching the masses.

For Francis and those who follow his path, spiritual growth isn't a solitary or selfish pleasure: Mystical union with God is part of a preparation for selfless service to the world.

> *When a tree grows by itself it spreads out, but does not grow tall. When trees grow together in the forest, they help push each other up towards the sun.*
> —BUDDHIST MONASTIC SAYING

OK. You're not ready to chuck everything and move to a monastery. There may even be traces of the John Wayne gene in your system, and you like your independence too much to give it all up and live communally. That's fine. God makes all kinds of people. But there are some lessons of community that you can apply in your life, no matter what kind of situation you live in.

First, may I suggest that you come visit us at the Brothers and Sisters of Charity at Little Portion Hermitage, or participate in a retreat at our nearby Little Portion Retreat and Training Center? We sponsor a number of retreats and gatherings covering a variety of topics and spiritual disciplines. And we'd love to have you join us.

If a trip to Arkansas isn't in your future, how about visiting one of the monasteries or Christian communities in your area? Even some of the most tightly closed communities have some kinds of regular activities or outreach that are open to the public. If you don't know where they are, call a local church office. Or you might want to get a copy of the fine *Sanctuaries* directories authored by Jack and Marcia Kelly, a husband-and-wife team who have spent years visiting, evaluating, and writing about America's many monasteries, guest houses, and retreat centers.

Visiting a community is like sampling a fine wine. One sip isn't enough to get tipsy, and one visit isn't enough time to experience the intoxicating intimacy with God and others that such living offers. But perhaps you can get a taste for how the community works, how its members worship and work together.

At the same time, be on the lookout for other ways of becoming part of a larger community. Many churches have small groups that are designed to help people apply their faith to their lives throughout the week. These groups vary widely. Some are oriented toward discussion and study. Others are more social. Still others are geared toward being places where individuals can work through various therapy and recovery issues. In addition, many regions have vibrant salons and book discussion groups, allowing people to gather, swap ideas, and grow their minds. Whatever style of group you want, there's probably one nearby. Also, look at your performance as a member of the communities you are already a part of.

The Catholic Church, like many other churches and non-Christian faiths, teaches that the nuclear family is the primary community of civilization. In fact, Confucianism teaches that if you want to save the empire you must first save the family. Are you a good father, mother, daughter, son, sister, brother, aunt, uncle, or grandparent? Or do family members see you as more wrapped up in your own life than you are in theirs? Think of ways you can love and serve your family members and strengthen the bonds of love between you all.

Think, too, about how you can reach out in love to the people next door, the coworker in the next cubicle, and the people you come into contact with day after day. Too many of us are invisible people, living in virtual isolation from those nearest to us.

Explore ways you can become involved in working for the common good in your community and country. Voting is considered kind of an entry-level act of civic responsibility. But you may also want to investigate other ways you can make a difference in the world. Maybe a group from your church, your workplace, or your neighborhood can get together to work on some needed community project.

Be devoted to one another in brotherly love. Honor one another above yourselves.—St. Paul

Independence is a pervasive and popular myth. But the truth is that nothing in our universe is truly independent. Nature is an interdependent network. The cosmos is communitarian.

God wants us to be more interdependent as well, not only for our own good but for the good of the world as well.

David Janzen, a member of Reba House, a Chicago-area Christian community, and the author of *Fire, Salt, and Peace*, a guidebook to Christian communities, argues that communities have a powerful influence on people, not only on those within their confines but on others as well: "On the eve of the new millennium, the Christian movement is growing again in response to God's timeless call, as a sign against the materialistic society that worships production and consumption without limit. In the years ahead, we cannot expect the social and political climate to favor community, but we can expect that many more will be seeking refuge under its roof, because the dominant society offers them no home and little meaning for their struggles."

An old revivalist hymn says, "This world is not my home, I'm just passing through." Likewise, an ancient monastic teaching describes life as a boat, with our fallen world as a rough sea, community as a place of calm, and heaven as the safe harbor to which we ultimately sail. For me, community helps make that passage from here to there feel a little more like home.

9

Compassion

❧

Everything people leave after them in this world is lost, but for their charity and almsgiving they will receive a reward from God.—FRANCIS

EACH AGE HAS ITS CELEBRITIES, ITS titans of business, its victors at war, its beautiful people. But rarely do the headlines or the gossip pages honor the humble, the sorrowful. That's what makes it so exciting when someone like Mother Teresa of Calcutta appears on the scene. Armed with nothing but compassion and caring, she suffered with the poor who lived and died in the streets of India, earning the Nobel Peace Prize in 1979 for her labors after decades of serving in silence and anonymity.

In many ways, it was the same with Francis of Assisi. The example of his life, along with his wise words, shows me that compassion isn't easy or painless, but may be life's most demanding work.

By compassion we make others' misery our own.
—SIR THOMAS BROWNE

I was settling into my seat on a 737, getting ready for another one of my frequent flights to Los Angeles, when an attractively dressed couple sat down next to me and struck up a conversation.

"What do you do?" the man asked. Dressed as I was in my brown habit and sandals, I felt sure he could tell I wasn't a high-powered corporate attorney working on a multimillion-dollar lawsuit, or a glamorous movie star on my way back to my Hollywood Hills mansion after weeks of filming my latest action feature.

I told him I was a Catholic musician on my way to a concert. He seemed to tense. I then asked him where he and his partner were going. He nervously told me that he and his wife were doctors, and they were on their way to speak at a national conference for abortion providers in L.A.

Before I tell you what happened next, hit the PAUSE button for a minute. Regardless of your position on abortion, which is probably one of the most complex and divisive moral issues of our time, imagine where this conversation could have gone.

Borrowing a few tactics from the militant antiabortion movement, I could have screamed: "MURDERERS!!!" I could have thumped a Bible, shouting, "God says thou shalt not kill!" I could have shown them grisly pictures of an aborted fetus. I could have done any number of things to hammer home the message that I was right and they were wrong, that I was on God's side and they were in league with the Devil, and that they were nasty sinners totally deserving of God's wrath.

But think for a minute. This man wasn't born yesterday, and if he'd been involved with abortion for more than a day he was probably well acquainted with the arguments raised against his work. In fact, there was a good chance his office had been picketed. Perhaps he had even received death threats from rabid pro-lifers! I could feel the man's obvious discomfort, along with his uncertainty about where the conversation was headed. I suspect he could probably sense when someone had moral objections to his profession, as I did.

OK. Hit the PLAY button again. Instead of judging this couple and delivering a blistering sermon on the evils of abortion, I simply asked them questions and listened to them. Before long we were having a cordial conversation about what got them involved in this work. Their defensiveness softened, their apprehension lifted, and they began to talk freely with me about some of their deepest feelings.

The woman almost cried as she told me about the horrors of seeing women give birth to malformed blobs of flesh that would live two or three minutes before dying in the maternity ward. She talked passionately about babies being born without limbs, faces, or brains. Hearing her didn't change my position, but it did change the way I looked at her, the way I related to her.

And because I was willing to listen instead of summarily condemning them, they shared with me how uncomfortable they were with where the abortion industry was going. They had grave concerns about the easy availability of abortion. They were saddened at how some women would come to their clinic for two, three, or even four abortions. And they were troubled by the fact that, in their minds, the scientific evidence was mounting that life begins at conception.

We wouldn't have had this conversation if I had rushed to judgment, which seems to be an all-too-common reaction among religious people these days. Around the world and in most major faith groups, a growing religious fundamentalism is reacting with righteous wrath against a perceived slide toward secularism and moral relativism. People argue, protest, do acts of violence, and even kill in an effort to promote what they believe to be God's will! Some even argue that talking as I did with known "enemies of God" is an act of cowardice and compromise.

Francis taught a different approach toward dealing with our conflicts and disagreements, an approach based on Jesus' life of compassion, charity, gentleness, and love. Francis didn't see the world in terms of good guys and bad guys, sinners and saints. He saw the world as being full of God's children, all of whom deserved love and respect.

Sinners are led back to God by holy meekness better than by cruel scolding.—FRANCIS

Crime was as big a problem in the Middle Ages as it is today. Then as now, people wanted to punish those who preyed on society. Getting tough on crime is a concept at least as old as the ancient maxim: "an eye for an eye and a tooth for a tooth." But the all-encompassing compassion of Francis led him down a radically different path, as we can see from the way he handled the issue of crime in a story from the *Little Flowers of St. Francis.*

During his endless travels, Francis preached in a village called Monte Casale, which was about fifty miles northwest of Assisi. Some there were touched by his message, and started a small community of friars. One day, three robbers who were notorious for their local crime sprees approached the community and asked for something to eat. Brother Angelo, the guardian of the community, scolded them and shooed them away. "You do not deserve that the earth should bear you up," he cried out. "So go about your business—and don't you ever come back here."

Later that same day, Francis visited the friars after begging alms in the area. When Brother Angelo told Francis about how he had protected the community from the robbers, Francis was horrified, and gave Brother Angelo a brief lesson in theology: "You acted in a cruel way, because sinners are led back to God by holy meekness better than by cruel scolding. For our Master Jesus Christ, whose gospel we have promised to observe, says that the doctor is not needed by those who are well but by the sick."

Francis didn't stop there. He ordered the friar to make amends with the robbers, saying, "So, since you acted against charity and against the example of Jesus Christ, I order you under holy obedience to take right now this sack of bread and jug of wine which I begged. Go and look carefully for those robbers over the mountains and valleys until you find them. And offer them this bread and this wine for me. And then kneel down before them and humbly accuse yourself of your sin of cruelty. And then ask them in my name not to do those evil things any more, but to fear God, and not to offend their neighbors. And if they do so, I promise them that I will supply them with provisions for their needs and I will give them food and drink all the time."

You can imagine the surprise of the robbers as they watched the friar who had shunned them approaching with bread and wine. They were accustomed to abuse. They knew how to react when they were rejected and condemned. But this unexpected display of grace caught them off guard. The compassion the friar showed them inspired them to consider the compassion of God, which they were convinced they didn't deserve. After Francis assured them that they could be forgiven for their sins and receive God's mercy, the three quit their lives of crime, devoted themselves to God, and joined the Franciscan movement.

Of course, not all criminals would take advantage of such grace. Nor was Francis making a sweeping public policy pronouncement against criminal statutes, courts, or incarceration. Francis wasn't "soft on crime," but his heart was unusually soft toward individual criminals who crossed his path. Instead of reacting with harsh judgmentalism, he acted with gentle grace. In many cases, his compassion touched hearts and changed lives.

If you forgive men when they sin against you, your heavenly Father will also forgive you. But if you do not forgive men their sins, your Father will not forgive your sins.—JESUS

Many of us spend much of our lives juggling a huge contradiction. On the one hand, we have a strong sense of right and wrong, and wonder why more people don't suffer the consequences of their actions. Why does the street criminal return to the street to rob again? Why does the slimy politician get reelected time after time? Why does the dishonest businessperson become filthy rich?

On the other hand, if you're like me, you regularly break "little" laws like speed limits, as well as your own internal moral code, and plead with the powers that be to let you off the hook just one more time. In other words, most of us want justice for others and mercy for ourselves.

But Francis taught a totally different approach. He didn't view the failures of others as occasions to ascend to the seat of judgment and render harsh verdicts on the world's evildoers. Instead, Francis taught that when others fall, we are to bend down and pick them up. Here's how he put it in his Rule: "All the friars . . . should be careful not to be upset or angry when anyone falls into sin or gives bad example; the Devil would be only too glad to ensnare many others through one man's sin. They are bound, on the contrary, to give the sinner spiritual aid, as best they can."

In *The Admonitions*, a collection of sayings compiled soon after his death, Francis reflected on the theme "compassion for one's neighbor": "Blessed the man who is patient with his neighbor's shortcomings as he would like him to be if he were in a similar position himself."

Jesus makes it clear: We can't have it both ways. We

can only receive forgiveness if we are willing to give it to others. If we can't forgive them, God isn't going to forgive us. Like a cosmic boomerang, the judgments we render on others will come back to us when God judges us.

It pains me to see the judgmentalism of those who call themselves followers of Jesus. I understand that attitude because that's where I was after I first converted to Christianity. I bristled with righteous indignation. I prided myself on my ability to cite biblical chapter and verse whenever someone made a minuscule moral misstep. My life was harsh and haughty, and I was devoid of God's grace.

That approach is all too common today. Listen carefully and you can hear Christians say these things:

"God hates fags."
"Lock the criminals up and throw away the key."
"Kick out those immigrants. After all, this is our country!"
"To vote for [fill in the blank] is a sin against God."

Too often, people who say they love God seem to lack the least bit of love for others. Francis would have understood. Loving the unlovable didn't come natural to him, either. He had to learn it the hard way.

Compassion is the sometimes fatal capacity for feeling what it's like to live inside somebody else's skin. It is the knowledge that there can never really be any peace and joy for me until there is peace and joy finally for you too.—FREDERICK BUECHNER

It wasn't until the late nineteenth century that doctors discovered the microscopic bacteria responsible for leprosy, a contagious disease that attacks the skin and the nerves, causing deformed features and nerve damage, as well as blindness and paralysis.

Before then, people often didn't know what to make of lepers. Was their ailment physiological, or was it caused by some kind of sin? Regardless of the cause, everyone pretty much thought it best to isolate lepers. For most of ancient and modern history, people with leprosy suffered alone in enclaves of the infected, shut off from everyone else. Though these sanctuaries were deemed holy by the church, most churches closed the doors of their hearts to them.

Francis grew up with a strong distaste for the sight and smell of lepers, with their oozing sores, foul rags, hideous faces, and stubby hands. As one biographer recalled, "So greatly loathsome was the sight of lepers to him . . . he would look at their houses only from a distance of two miles and he would hold his nostrils with his hands."

But as Francis began to turn his heart and his mind over to God, things began to change. One day when Francis was riding down a road near Assisi he saw a leper approaching from a distance. He felt all the familiar feelings—the discomfort, the fear, the nausea, the desire to flee—as the lonely leper came closer and closer. But Francis, ennobled and enabled by God's grace, got down off his mule, walked up to the leper, and kissed him.

"When I was in sins, it seemed extremely bitter to

me to look at lepers," recalled the saint, "and the Lord himself led me among them and I practiced mercy with them." Soon, Francis was living at a leprosy hospital, caring for the lepers' needs and washing their wounds. And as Francis's movement grew, many of the friars lived with and served lepers, whom they called "our Christian brothers."

But something deeper happened that day Francis first kissed the leper. A line had been crossed. Listening to his heart instead of his fears, he had ventured out beyond his comfort zone and reached out to another in love and compassion. And having done so this once, it became easier to do so again and again. Soon he learned to express the same charity toward the chronically poor, the socially outcast, the lonely, the insane, and others. Gradually, the love of God overflowed in his life and that love overcame his self-protection. These small victories changed the direction of his movement, and of human history.

> *They should be glad to live among social outcasts, among the poor and helpless, the sick and the lepers, and those who beg by the wayside.*
> —EARLY RULE OF ST. FRANCIS

Francis's Rule for his order turned popular prejudices on their heads. Instead of "networking" with the rich, the powerful, the famous, and the beautiful, he made a beeline for the poor, the weak, the downtrodden, and the forgotten—those unfortunate souls who were considered ugly in the eyes of everyone but God (who had made them) and Francis (who loved them).

Francis wasn't blind or deluded. He wasn't oblivious to people's misfortune, nor was he a romantic idealist. The only explanation for his bizarre behavior is this: He could see God's divine spark in all people, no matter how far down on their luck they were. Or as St. Bonaventure put it, "In every poor person he met, he saw the image of Christ and he insisted on giving them anything which had been given to him."

In a sense, Francis was the Mother Teresa of his day. Every time he looked at a poor person, his heart saw Jesus, who himself came from a poor family, was rejected by those he came to save, and was condemned to death as a common criminal. For St. Francis, as for Mother Teresa, the heart of love transubstantiated the poor and the lowly into the image bearers of God Almighty.

When he saw a poor person, Francis didn't judge ("What a worthless individual!"). He didn't evaluate ("I wonder what kind of bad work habits and poor social skills got him into this mess?"). He didn't turn his head or try to pass by on the other side of the road. He loved and reached out in compassion and charity.

About the only people Francis couldn't love were those who scorned and ridiculed the poor and oppressed. "He bore it very ill if he saw a poor person reproached or if he heard a curse hurled upon any creature by anyone," wrote Thomas of Celano. Brother Thomas also observed that Francis's compassion for others was more than an issue in the mind; it was a matter of the heart: "He transferred to himself the afflictions of all who were sick." According to other biographers, Francis emphasized charity over book learning. Although study and scholarship were favored activities among other monastic orders, Francis felt study without compassionate activity allowed too many Christians to "remain inwardly cold and empty."

Francis preached a message of poverty and simplicity, but he forbade his brothers to look down on the rich: "I warn all the friars and exhort them not to condemn or look down on people whom they see wearing soft or gaudy clothes and enjoying luxuries in food or drink." And even though he preached a message of spiritual passion and purity, he honored and respected sinful and hypocritical priests, whom he upheld as servants of God.

As G. K. Chesterton said, "There was never a man who looked into those brown burning eyes without being certain that Francis was really interested in *him*; in his own inner individual life from the cradle to the grave; that he himself was being valued and taken seriously, and not merely added to the spoils of some social policy or the names in some clerical document."

"Love one another as I have loved you," said Jesus. Francis took him at his word in a way that was as rare as it was beautiful.

If we don't accept Jesus in one another, we will not be able to give Him to others.—MOTHER TERESA

One of the most revealing windows into a person's soul is the way she treats the outcast. Is the homeless person sleeping in the doorway seen as an eyesore and an annoyance, or as a human being deserving of kindness and care? Is the street person who reeks of alcohol and asks for a quarter brushed aside with disdain, or treated with a respect inspired by the realization that "There but for the grace of God go I"?

One of things that touched the people who lived and traveled with Francis was his gentleness to the least and the lowliest. "He showed all mildness to all men," said one biographer. Another observed: "He seemed to have a mother's tenderness in caring for the sufferings of those in misery." No living creature could escape Francis's relentless affection. "He overflowed with tender compassion even for animals, because to some extent he had returned to the state of innocence," wrote St. Bonaventure.

Of course, we expect such behavior from someone honored by the church as a saint. But what about the rest of us? Are compassion and charity for saints only, while the rest of us selfishly look out first and foremost for ourselves?

Francis would never buy that. He believed everyone could practice a life of humility and gentleness. That's why he wrote it into his Rule for his friars to follow: "And this is my advice, my counsel, and my earnest plea to my friars in our Lord Jesus Christ that, when they travel about the world, they should not be quarrelsome or take part in disputes with words or criticize others; but they should be gentle, peaceful, and unassuming, courteous and humble, speaking respectfully to everyone, as is expected of them."

Love does not give money, it gives itself. If it gives itself first and a lot of money too, that is all the better. But first it must sacrifice itself.—THOMAS MERTON

Francis was a poor man with few earthly possessions: a simple tunic, a rope belt, and some sandals. But that didn't stop him from being a lavish giver. Whenever anyone asked him for help, he gave anything he could, showing that generosity is a matter of the size of the heart, not the size of the gift.

So willing was Francis to give anything he had, so reluctant to grasp anything as his own to possess, that it was only through the perseverance of his followers that Francis avoided a life full of nakedness and cold. He gave away his tunic more often than most of the brothers could remember. Friends and neighbors who saw Francis wandering around partially clothed would give him tunics, mantles, and other pieces of clothing to protect him from the elements. But this was futile. Francis would give these garments away as soon as he was asked, treating them as temporary loans rather than permanent possessions.

Once when he was fortunate enough to be wearing a pair of trousers, he gave even those away when some needy soul asked! And if Francis was out of clothes to give, he offered to help others by begging alms in their behalf or working alongside them in a field and giving them the money.

Even the humble adornments in the brothers' simple chapel were given away. Once when a poor woman came to the friars begging for help, they searched and found nothing they could give her. Francis thought otherwise: "We have one New Testament," he said. "Give the New Testament to our mother that she might sell it to take care of her needs, since we are admonished by it to help the poor. I believe indeed that the gift of it will be more pleasing to God than our reading from it."

Although some religious folks may accuse Francis of sacrilege, and in other places he stresses adorning the altar with greater dignity, he preferred to stand guilty before human accusers than disappoint God with a miserly spirit. "Give alms," said Francis, "because they wash away the stains of sin from our souls."

> *If I give all I possess to the poor and surrender my body to the flames, but have not love, I gain nothing.*
> —ST. PAUL

I had always been uneasy when poor people came up to me and asked me for money. It would have been easiest to give them money and be done with it, but I was concerned about where the money would go. In some cases, I felt sure it would buy drugs or cheap wine.

Then a friend showed me a better way. A dirty man who smelled like a brewery approached him and asked for money, but instead of giving cash or shooing the man away, my friend asked the man if he would like a sandwich or a cup of coffee instead. "Sure!" said the shocked beggar, who walked into a fast food restaurant with my friend and walked out with a sandwich, a soft drink, and a blessing.

I watched as the man disappeared down the crowded sidewalk, clutching his burger and soda. That food was probably gone in minutes, but I believe my friend's act of selfless giving will last for all eternity. It took an investment of only a few minutes and a few dollars to make that simple gesture of genuine love and concern. This episode opened my eyes to how many of the same simple opportunities surround us nearly every time we walk down a crowded urban street.

There's nothing romantic about poverty. The first time you pick someone up off the street who's lying in his own urine and vomit, your romanticism dissipates pretty quickly. But it was more than romantic idealism that inspired Francis and his band of brothers.

> *We can never love our neighbor too much. There is nothing small in the service of God.*
>
> —St. Francis de Sales

Most major faiths preach compassion, even though they differ about what it means. For Francis, compassion is inspired by the example of Jesus and by the mystical presence of Christ in every human being. But for Buddhists, compassion is seen as a way to break down the illusory barriers separating human from human and keeping all from union with the Ultimate.

We can debate such differences forever, but that's precisely where too many people stop. Compassion, if it has any meaning at all, needs to be translated into action.

I'm repeatedly struck by the fact Francis couldn't be truly compassionate until he confronted his abhorrence of lepers. Prior to kissing the leper on the road, Francis was bound-up, self-contained, and compassion-challenged. But with God's help, he was able to love that leper. The rest came naturally.

God wants to help you know that kind of love. What about it? What is it that keeps you from being more compassionate? What protective barriers have you erected around your life to keep you from seeing the pain of others, hearing their cries of need, or reaching out to them in love and blessing?

And who are the lepers you need to reach out to? Open your eyes and your heart as you drive your car or walk through town. Perhaps God is calling you to love someone you consider unlovable.

One way to show compassion and grow in your love for others is to practice the discipline of listening. Instead of focusing on yourself and your own concerns and troubles, try getting inside someone else's skin by hearing them deeply, earnestly, and lovingly.

While listening to another, resist the all-too-human urge to critique what is being said. Compassion isn't about whether you approve or disapprove of what someone is saying; it's about understanding another person. It isn't about promoting your agenda; it's about comprehending someone else's.

If you truly and sympathetically hear another person, the things being said will travel into your ears, through your brain, and straight to your heart, where your emotions will be touched. As you practice the discipline of listening, you'll go beyond relating to others on a superficial intellectual level and begin feeling what they feel. In time, laughing with those who laugh and weeping with those who weep will become second nature to you. But feeling what others feel will never be possible if you don't listen.

After you've learned how to hear one or two people at close range, try expanding your ear to your neighborhood and your community. Listen as people express their complaints and grievances, hearing between the lines for their deepest cries of need and longing.

> *You should bear patiently the bad temper of other people, the slights, the rudeness that may be offered you.*—St. John Bosco

Perhaps you need to begin by forgiving someone who has hurt you in the past. An unforgiving spirit blocks the flow of grace and mercy into our lives, causing us to drown in a stagnant cesspool of regrets, animosities, and grudges.

Who do you need to forgive? Is it a parent or sibling who slighted you? Is it a friend or lover who hurt you? Is it a priest, pastor, or teacher who took advantage of a position of trust and authority? Is it a kamikaze driver on the freeway who terrorizes your morning commute? A telemarketer who invades your dinner hour?

Forgiving someone doesn't mean that what they did was right. As Frederick Buechner writes, forgiveness is a way of saying: "You have done something unspeakable, and by all rights I should call it quits between us. Both my pride and my principles demand no less. However, although I make no guarantees that I will be able to forget what you've done and though we both may carry the scars for life, I refuse to let it stand between us. I still want you for my friend."

Forgiveness simply means getting down off the seat of judgment and releasing those who have offended you from your own hostility and anger.

And while you're at it, ask God to forgive you for the

ways you've let down him and others. Freed by forgiveness and energized by love, you can be a channel of charity, compassion, and grace in a hard and needy world.

10

Creation

꧁꧂

🕊 *Every creature in heaven and on earth and in the depths of the sea should give God praise and glory and honor and blessing.*—FRANCIS

OUTSIDE THE SLIDING GLASS DOOR OF my small hermitage at Little Portion is a bird feeder, which I keep stocked with corn and seeds. From morning to dusk, dozens of redbirds, cardinals, bluebirds, finches, and orioles stop to eat at that feeder. Regardless of whether it's the middle of winter and I'm stuck inside looking out, or whether it's in the dog days of summer and Viola and I are out tending our garden, those beautiful birds visit, giving us a tiny glimpse into the wonders of nature.

Often, as I sit watching the birds and meditating, I enter a state of reverie in which I find myself experiencing deep feelings of love for nature and nature's God. At those moments, I feel particularly close to the spirit of Francis, who is honored by the Catholic Church as the patron saint of animals and the environment.

I have felt a deep closeness to nature for as long as I

can remember. I grew up in a farm area where I was continually surrounded and amazed by the natural world.

During the 1960s and 1970s, a time when many people
throughout the Western world were waking up to the
problems of pollution and environmental degradation,
the band I was in, Mason Proffit, sang out about the
exploitation of nature in songs like "500 Men." At the
time, it was extremely easy to be critical of large companies that unnecessarily contaminated the environment.
But the more I thought about it, the more critical I grew
of you and me—the millions of consumers whose endless search for everything new and shiny helped cause
this continual onslaught on nature.

I came to believe that the "American way of life" was
a major part of the problem. I looked to churches and
religious leaders to raise questions about consumerism
and the never-ending desire for more and more of bigger and better goods. But it seemed that religion merely
baptized consumerism, legitimized humanity's dominion
over nature, and fueled the mindless exploitation of
creation.

If anything, my fifteen years spent following in the
footsteps of Francis have made me even more concerned
about caring for creation. During that time I have come
to see that it's not the Christian faith that supported and
blessed humanity's rapacious ways. Instead, Christianity
was distorted, and these distorted doctrines were used to
justify human greed. There's still plenty of distortion
around, and one can still find people quoting the Bible
to back up their view that nature is here for us to use and
abuse in just about any way we see fit.

That wasn't the kind of faith that Francis followed.

My brothers, birds, you should praise your Creator very much and always love him.—FRANCIS

Mother Teresa's best-known speech is an address she gave to the United Nations. Globe-trotting evangelist Billy Graham made history when he preached behind the Iron Curtain during the height of the Cold War. St. Francis was a tireless preacher who introduced thousands of people to the Christian message and founded a world-wide order. But Francis's most famous sermon is one he gave to a flock of birds, and this singular event explains why Francis is now enshrined in millions of bird feeders around the world.

One day Francis and some friars were traveling through the Spoleto valley near Bevagna. Looking up and seeing the trees full of doves, crows, and daws, Francis "left his companions in the road and ran eagerly toward the birds" and "humbly begged them to listen to the word of God."

One of the friars recorded the sermon, which overflows with Francis's love for creation and its Creator: "My brothers, birds, you should praise your Creator very much and always love him; he gave you feathers to clothe you, wings so that you can fly, and whatever else was necessary for you. God made you noble among his creatures, and he gave you a home in the purity of the air; though you neither sow nor reap, he nevertheless protects and governs you without any solicitude on your part."

Thomas of Celano records that the birds stretched their necks and extended their wings as Francis walked among them touching and blessing them. This event was a turning point of sorts for Francis. "He began to blame himself for negligence in not having preached to the birds before" and "from that day on, he solicitously admonished all birds, all animals and reptiles, and even creatures that have no feeling, to praise and love their Creator."

Francis's brief encounter with those birds heightened the saint's already profound enchantment with all of God's creation, and for the remainder of his life, Francis loved and looked after birds, some of whom provided him with companionship at his private cell, some of whom he rescued from hunters' snares, and some of whom he silenced when their noisy song interrupted his saying of the Mass!

Centuries after the death of Francis, his hometown of Assisi still honors his affection for winged creatures. There, as in other towns, church bells ring three times a day to announce the Angelus, an ancient Christian prayer that honors the incarnation of Jesus. But in Assisi, the reciting of this prayer is accompanied by the feeding of the saint's beloved birds.

And it's not just Assisi that honors Francis's deep love for creation. Every year on the Sunday nearest his October 4 feast day, thousands of Catholic, Episcopalian, and Protestant churches around the world host services where animals are blessed. Some people still can't get over the sight of people bringing their dogs, cats, and even horses into a church, or a nearby churchyard, but these services are a powerful way to celebrate both Francis's and God's compassionate concern for all creatures.

Many of these ceremonies include Francis's "Canticle of Brother Sun." Written late in the saint's life when blindness had cut him off from the outside world, the canticle shows that his imagination was aflame with love for creation.

$\mathcal{M}$ost high, all-powerful, all good, Lord!
   All praise is yours, all glory, all honor
   And all blessing.
To you, alone, Most High, do they belong.
   No mortal lips are worthy
   To pronounce your name.
All praise be yours, my Lord, through all that
     you have made,
   And first my lord Brother Sun,
   Who brings the day; and light you to give to us
     through him.
How beautiful is he, how radiant in all his splendor!
   Of you, Most High, he bears the likeness.
All praise be yours, my Lord, through Sister Moon
     and Stars;
   In the heavens you have made them, bright
   And precious and fair.
All praise be yours, my Lord, through Brothers
     Wind and Air,
   And fair and stormy, all the weather's moods,
   By which you cherish all that you have made.
All praise be yours, my Lord, through Sister Water,
   So useful, lowly, precious and pure.
All praise be yours, my Lord, through Brother Fire,
   Through whom you brighten up the night.

How beautiful is he, how gay! Full of power
   and strength.
All praise be yours, my Lord, through Sister
   Earth, our mother,
   Who feeds us in her sovereignty and produces
   Various fruits with colored flowers and herbs.
All praise be yours, my Lord, through those
   who grant pardon
   For love of you; through those who endure
   Sickness and trial.
Happy those who endure in peace,
   By you, Most High, they will be crowned.
All praise be yours, my Lord, through Sister Death,
   From whose embrace no mortal can escape.
Woe to those who die in mortal sin!
   Happy those she finds doing your will!
   The second death can do no harm to them.
Praise and bless my Lord, and give him thanks,
   And serve him with great humility.

❧

The key to understanding this unusual saint's unique
approach to the cosmos is this: If God made it, Francis
adored it. All created things were a part of God's big
family, and through the adoration of the things God had
made, Francis felt an exhilaration that was both rooted
and soaring, both worldly and spiritual.

*It's important to treat animals well. It is the hall-
mark of our entire society. If we treat animals badly,
we probably treat each other badly.*—ROGER CARAS

Francis wasn't a political activist, but there was one problem so urgent and widespread that he felt it required government intervention, and that was the abuse of animals. Whenever he saw a farmer beating a horse, a hunter snaring a bird, or the citizens of a town allowing dogs to starve to death, Francis grew intensely sad. Boldly and repeatedly he petitioned various government officials to enact laws against such cruelty toward animals: "If I could talk to the emperor, I would beg him, for the love of God, to grant my prayer and to publish an edict forbidding anyone from trapping our sisters the larks or from inflicting any harm on them. Furthermore . . . all the lords of castles and of villages ought to oblige their subjects every year on the day of the Nativity of the Lord to throw wheat or other grain on the roads [so that] the birds and especially our sisters the larks would have food . . . and that everyone be obliged to give our brothers the oxen and the asses a generous amount of feed."

The concern of Francis for God's creatures was never enacted into law, but it has endeared him to generations of friends of the earth, including Lynn White Jr., a historian who is an otherwise harsh critic of Christianity's role in the environmental crisis. In Francis, White saw a saint whose theology of creation was an exception to centuries of church-sanctioned exploiting and plundering of nature. White wrote an article suggesting that Francis be named the patron saint of ecology, and the Vatican officially recognized Francis with that title on Easter Sunday in 1980.

But animals have known that Francis was their patron for centuries. As one biographer wrote: "It is indeed wonderful how even irrational creatures recognized his affection for them and felt his tender love for them."

We have forgotten how to be good guests, how to walk lightly on the earth as its other creatures do.
  —STATEMENT OF 1972 STOCKHOLM ENVIRONMENTAL
  CONFERENCE, "ONLY ONE EARTH"

The life of Francis was punctuated by rapturous celebrations of the joys of creation and ceaseless efforts to protect all creatures from suffering or harm.

Traveling one day near Greccio, the town where he had enlisted animals in the world's first Christmas crèche, the saint came upon a rabbit that had been caught in a trap. Francis freed the animal, saying, "Brother rabbit, come to me." The rabbit jumped into his arms, where it stayed until the saint instructed it to go back to its hutch.

Outside Rieti Francis saw a man who had caught a number of fish, which Francis "threw back into the water, commanding them to be careful lest they be caught again." While walking, Francis often stopped to give roadside assistance to worms that were wriggling across the road. "He picked them up from the road and placed them in a safe place, lest they should be crushed by the feet of passersby."

Francis loved honey and often praised the amazing work of bees. He tried to look out for the bees, seeing that they "would be provided with honey in the winter, or the best wine."

Likewise, the saint befriended the mice that ran through the sleeping area he shared with his friars, developed a mutually beneficial relationship with a falcon who woke Francis for prayer every night, and provided shelter to a cicada who joined him in singing God's praises for a week.

But Francis's affection didn't stop with the animals who lived and breathed, but extended to all elements of creation. He saw God's exquisite handiwork in everything: "He forbade the brother(s) to throw embers of half-burned logs to the winds, as is customarily done: he wanted them to be placed gently on the ground out of respect for Him who created them. . . . He did not even want them to extinguish a candle, a lamp, or fire, as one does when it is no longer needed, so great was his tenderness and pity for that creature. Once when his drawers caught fire, Francis stopped a brother who had rushed to put them out: "No, my dearest brother, don't harm our Brother Fire."

Francis was to reach out to Brother Fire again, near the end of his life. Suffering from near blindness, Francis was told by the medical experts of his day that his temples should be cauterized with a glowing iron. As the red-hot iron approached his face, Francis said this simple prayer:

"Brother Fire, the Most High has made thee most strong, beautiful and useful beyond all other elements. Be merciful, then, to me in this hour, be kind, because I have always loved thee in God."

Those who watched the barbaric procedure marveled as Francis calmly endured an experience that forced some to black out from pain. "I assure you that I felt neither the torture of the fire nor any other pain," he said.

I could fill a book with the stories—and a menagerie with the creatures—that reveal Francis's love for creation. Instead, I'll rest with the word of Thomas of Celano: "Who could ever give expression to the very great affection he bore for all things that are God's? Who would be able to narrate the sweetness he enjoyed while contemplating in creatures the wisdom of their Creator, his power and his goodness? Indeed, he was often filled with a wonderful and ineffable joy from this consideration while he looked upon the sun, while he beheld the moon, and while he gazed upon the stars and the firmament."

> *If you wish to know the Divine, feel the wind on your face and the warm sun on your hand.*—BUDDHA

Francis loved all of creation, but he loved God more, and his affection for some creatures was heavily influenced by biblical symbols, as one biographer points out: "Among all the various kinds of animals, he loved little lambs with a special predilection and more ready affection, because in the sacred scriptures the humility of our Lord Jesus Christ is more frequently likened to that of the lamb."

As a result, Francis was particularly nettlesome to merchants who were anything less than gentle while taking lambs to market. "Why are you torturing my brother lambs tied up and hanging like this?" he asked one merchant. But Francis's anger didn't lead him to boycott the lamb market. Rather, he and the friars were good for business, frequently buying animals at market and giving them to people who would care for them as family pets.

Even though Francis wasn't a vegetarian, he refused to eat lamb meat. "God forbid," he said. But he did enjoy wearing lamb's wool (at least until he gave his clothing away to someone more needy).

More unusual was the saint's reverence for inanimate objects, which he associated with God's animating love: "He walked reverently upon stones, because of him who was called the Rock," wrote one biographer.

Francis's love for nature was real, not symbolic. At the same time, his affection for some creatures was influenced by his affection for Jesus, whose parables and lessons frequently cited objects from the physical world to illustrate spiritual points.

> *To see a world in a grain of sand*
> *And a heaven in a wild flower,*
> *Hold infinity in the palm of your hand*
> *And eternity in an hour.*
> —WILLIAM BLAKE

Francis loved God so much that he wanted all of creation to join him in his celebration. That's the reason for his frequent sermons to nonhuman audiences, such as the one he delivered to a brightly colored field of flowers: "He preached to them and invited them to praise the Lord as if they were endowed with reason."

Francis wasn't out of his mind, nor was his behavior some kind of quaint, primitive, medieval, and ultimately silly anthropomorphism. Francis wasn't pretending that nature had human characteristics. Instead, he was urging all of creation to follow God in its own unique fashion: "In the same way he exhorted with the sincerest purity cornfields and vineyards, stones and forests and all the beautiful things of the fields, fountains of water and the green things of the gardens, earth and fire, air and wind, to love God and serve him willingly."

Over the past few decades, Francis has been enlisted as the poster boy for a whole series of theories and causes he wouldn't have supported. Pantheists (who believe that God is one and the same as nature), New Age or pagan-based nature worshipers (who see trees and rocks as inherently sacred), and Gaia theorists (who describe the cosmos as a living, breathing entity) have all claimed the saint's endorsement. This is certainly an honor to Francis and the Franciscans, who try to find common ground with all people of goodwill, but Francis was an ortho-dox theist who believed that God and nature were sepa-rate, though related.

Francis believed in a God who existed long before the universe did, and then created that universe out of nothing. Unlike some pantheists, who believe God would cease to exist if nature disappeared, Francis believed in a personal and powerful God who existed before anything else, and will continue to exist long after the physical uni-verse vanishes. Unlike pagans, who see holiness in every-thing that is, Francis saw holiness in God alone, but at the same time he honored and respected nature as amaz-ingly, even miraculously, good. Unlike Gaians, who see humanity and nature as part of one living system, Francis saw humans as uniquely endowed by God with spiritu-ality, or souls, but he didn't strip away nature's dignity, and he stressed how people and creatures are inextricably linked. Of course, you don't have to subscribe to Francis's belief system to appreciate him or learn from his example. Anyone can respect and benefit from this saint's love for the cosmos.

Likewise, various groups of animal rights activists have tried to enlist Francis in their battles. I feel certain that Francis would join them in condemning the abuse of animals. Francis invited creatures to praise God, which seems to suggest he believed animals could experience both joy and pain. Consequently, I am convinced that he would condemn the inhumane conditions that exist in many large agribusiness facilities, where animals are confined to tiny compartments for all of their brief and unhappy lives.

It's true that Francis rarely ate meat, but that's because of his desire to live a life of simplicity and poverty, not because he was a vegetarian. And Francis rarely rode on donkeys or horses, but that's because he usually offered a ride to someone who was walking. He never claimed that people couldn't use animals, only that they shouldn't abuse these beautiful creatures of God. But Francis wouldn't agree with those segments of the animal rights movement that claim there's no difference between animals and humans, or that humans have no right to eat meat and use other animal products. Putting animals and humans on the same level won't necessarily guarantee that humans will begin treating animals better. And as some thinkers have argued, such moral equivalency may only serve to complicate already complex social issues like euthanasia and the rationing of limited medical care.

In everything created, Francis saw the handiwork of the Creator. Therefore, to disrespect creation was to disrespect God. That didn't make creation and God the same thing, but it means the two are closely related.

Perhaps more than any other saint, Francis understood what was meant when God told Adam and Eve in the opening chapter of Genesis to "be fruitful and increase in number; fill the earth and subdue it." In the King James Version of the Bible, which has been read for centuries, "subdue" was translated as "have dominion." Unfortunately, many people thought "dominion" meant exploitation and abuse. Francis believed instead in the notion of "domestication," meaning that we can prune a tree to make it grow more fully, or train an animal so it works together with us. But he would never let dominion become "domineering," where we use creatures for our own good with no respect for the life and feelings of the creature.

For Francis, caring for creation meant loving it the way a boy loves a puppy, or the way a girl loves a horse, not using it the way an ivory poacher massacres an elephant in order to get at its tusks.

Earth, with her thousand voices, praises God.
—SAMUEL TAYLOR COLERIDGE

The friars who followed Francis during his life and then wrote about him after his death often became excited as they described their beloved brother. When you stumble upon one of these passages in his biographies, you recognize that they're full of elation and soaring prose which sings across the centuries.

The various lives of Francis contain many passages about the saint's lifelong love affair with creation, like this one from Thomas of Celano's second life of the saint titled "Of the Contemplation of the Creator in His Creatures": "In every work of the artist he praised the Artist; whatever he found in the things made he referred to the Maker. He rejoiced in all the works of the hands of the Lord and saw behind things pleasant to behold their life-giving reason and cause. In beautiful things he saw Beauty itself; all things were to him good."

That doesn't mean that all things were perfect. Francis often saw greediness in animals, and occasionally he saw it punished. Once when the brothers were feeding some birds, they noticed how one large bird "persecuted" the other birds, driving them away from the food. This belligerent bird suffered for his misdeeds: "The disturber of his brothers got up on a vessel of water to drink and immediately fell into the water and suffocating, died."

Another time, Francis helped out the people of Gubbio, who were terrified of a fierce wolf who had killed their livestock and even some of their fellow villagers. According to the *Little Flowers*, Francis negotiated a settlement between the villagers and the angry animal.

"Come to me, Brother Wolf," said Francis. Once he got the animal's attention, he counseled him to adapt a more humane manner. "Brother Wolf, you have done great harm in this region, and you have committed horrible crimes by destroying God's creatures without any mercy." Francis brokered a deal in which the wolf would quit his attacks and the villagers would provide him with food, thus assuring that he would be well fed.

Francis didn't worship nature, which he saw as imperfect in some ways, just as human nature so clearly is. But he did worship God, and he cherished nature as if it were

God's love notes to an often lost and lonely people. And his life contains many wise principles we can use to heal the rift between creatures and their Creator.

> *The kiss of the sun for pardon,*
> *The song of the birds for mirth.*
> *One is nearer God's heart in a garden*
> *Than anywhere else on earth.*
>
> —DOROTHY GURNEY

Often when the birds are eating at the feeder outside my door, I greet them, saying, "Hello, sisters. Come to the harmony of God's love." It's a practice that feels perfectly comfortable and natural here at Little Portion, but which might cause people to wonder if I tried it in a city park or a zoo! Still, there are plenty of ways you can apply the Franciscan tradition in your particular situation and enjoy the benefits of a deeper appreciation of creation.

First off, begin by relating to our sisters the birds. If you're not already doing so, start feeding our feathered friends. Bird feeding and bird watching are becoming increasingly popular leisure activities, and it's a good thing because many birds are fighting for their lives as their forests are cut down and pesticides enter their food supplies. Feeding birds also provides plenty of time for prayer and reflection on the mysteries of God and the wonder of creation.

Many stores in your area have feeders, birdseed, and anything else you need to get started. And you can supplement their diet with bread, cornflakes, or other items that otherwise would have wound up in the trash. Once the birds in your neighborhood become aware that you want to feed them, they'll repay you with hours of fun and frenetic entertainment.

Another simple way to practice reverence for creation is to grow a garden. There's nothing like getting your hands in the dirt to put you in touch with nature, plus you get to experience exciting side benefits like back pain and sunburn!

Maybe you can't have a large garden like ours, which provides some of our own organically grown produce. We have corn, vegetables, fruits, and herbs, which we fertilize with our own "home-grown" animal manure. But even if you live in a New York City high-rise you can start a window box. And everyone can learn to grow houseplants. Whether you grow flowers or tomatoes, the process is all a part of knowing more about the wonderful world we inhabit.

A man who has lost his sense of wonder is a man dead.—WILLIAM OF SAINT-THIERRY

Seize the opportunity to walk in a park or drive through a forest with the windows down. As you're there in the midst of God's green earth, practice mindfulness, which is a way of meditating on what you see and the Creator who makes it possible. Breathe in the aromas that surround you. Quiet your heart and be aware that every step you take is on holy ground. Tune into the symphony of the birds and the rustle of the wind through the leaves. Thank God for the beauty of creation, which includes you!

If you want to decrease humanity's often harmful

impact on the world, try to consume less. Don't buy the lie of our mass-produced, throwaway culture. People in the industrialized West go through more of the world's precious resources than anyone else on the globe. Cut down on your consumption and purchases. Don't waste paper, which destroys forests and depletes the world's supply of oxygen. Focus on needs instead of wants. Simplify!

Recycle anything you can, including yard wastes. Cut your grass with a mulching mower instead of piling bags full of clippings on the curb for the trash man. Create a compost pile and use your yard wastes to fertilize your garden. Use detergents and other products that are biodegradable. And think about driving your current car for another year instead of trading it in for a newer model.

When you buy an appliance or tool, get the model that uses less energy. Try the 75-watt lightbulbs instead of the 150-watt bulbs, or better yet convert to fluorescent lights, which use 25 percent of the energy of standard bulbs. Use a hand-operated can opener instead of an electric model. When your water heater goes out, replace it with an energy-efficient model, even if it costs a few more dollars.

Take some of the money you'll be saving on energy and give it to groups that protect the environment, save the rain forests, or slow the disappearance of animal and plant species from the face of the earth. Take your kids to local zoos and arboretums, where they can observe some of the diversity of the animal and plant world and participate in classes about God's creatures. Support these organizations with your time and money.

Don't buy products that come from the exploitation

of animals, such as ivory or tortoiseshell jewelry or pianos with ivory keys. In fact, most of these items are banned from sale, as are products which require the killing of members of endangered species. Consider not buying that fur jacket.

> *I am a passenger on the spaceship Earth.*
> —R. BUCKMINSTER FULLER

Spaceship Earth is in trouble. The world's population is growing rapidly, and the dramatic shift of people from rural areas to huge urban centers threatens to overload our life support systems. The future of civilization may depend on new countercultural communities that restore the healthy balance between humans and creation. Integrated monastic communities like the Brothers and Sisters of Charity are more than havens for prayer and spiritual growth; they are outposts of a needed return to the basic rhythms of nature.

Perhaps you are being called to make a radical break with modern consumer society, which has brutalized nearly everything it has touched. If so, join the creation-friendly counterculture, which seeks to heal the world through ancient and time-tested principles.

11
Service

 God in His mercy has called us unto the salvation not only of our souls but of many.—FRANCIS

THE HISTORY OF WESTERN MONASTICISM CAN be divided into two distinct periods: pre-Francis and post-Francis. Prior to Francis, most monasteries and other religious communities were seen as holy refuges, places of sacred solitude, islands of spiritual calm in an often turbulent world. True, some monasteries sent out missionaries or evangelists, but the primary focus was on life within the enclosure walls. Francis changed that emphasis by striking a radically new balance between solitude and service, between separation from the world and intense dedication to it, between silent contemplation and active involvement in the messy hustle and bustle of everyday life.

Francis found his inspiration in the life of Jesus, whose love for us led him to become one of us by being born into the human race instead of remaining in heaven, aloof from us and all our problems.

Most Christians celebrate the Incarnation of Christ as man around Christmastime and ignore it for the rest of the year. But for Francis, the Incarnation served as a minute-by-minute reminder to be deeply involved in the world, loving people at close range instead of from inside the strong, stony walls of a monastery.

But don't get me wrong. Francis wasn't all work and no pray. The saint would devote hours of each day to pouring his heart out to God and seeking divine guidance for every facet of his life. He and the other friars also observed weekly fasts and regular periods of total isolation, which enabled them to recharge their spiritual batteries after days of caring for people's physical and spiritual needs. Here also they followed the pattern of Jesus, who balanced intense contemplation with loving service to the world. Jesus often retreated from the crowds who surrounded him, going to lonely, isolated spots to spend time alone with God. Once he spent forty days fasting and praying in the desert.

Francis understood that the dichotomy between solitude and service is a false one, because everyone needs both. If we don't spend time alone with God, we become spiritually weak, and our work in the world carries little of lasting value. On the other hand, if we spend all our time with God and never venture out into the world, we may become spiritually isolated and self-contained. We may be full of wonderful wisdom and divine power, but if we don't share that with others, who benefits? Certainly not other people, and often, not even ourselves.

Here's how saints down through the ages have

explained it: Contemplation and prayer are like an oasis in a dry desert. Through prayer, we store up a huge reservoir of water. Our service is the conduit for delivering the water. But once our reservoir is depleted, we need to return to our oasis so we don't wind up stranded in the desert without water. This is a picture of the life-giving balance between prayer and service.

Francis didn't start out intending to create a movement. When he realized that a movement was growing up around him, he struggled to find the proper balance between solitude and service, prayer and preaching. He also asked others to pray and seek an answer to the dilemma he faced. "What does my Lord Jesus Christ order me to do?" he asked.

Both Brother Masseo and Sister Clare were enlisted in Francis's intense search for God's guidance on the issue, and both received the same answer, which Brother Masseo reported to Francis: "He wants you to go about the world preaching, because God did not call you for yourself alone but also for the salvation of others."

Likewise, God has called all of us to find our own unique balance between solitude and service. My prayer is that the following pages can help you find yours.

Recall the life of Christ, especially the Passion, with vivid imagination.—ST. BONAVENTURE

It was around the time of Francis—a period which some call the dawning of the Renaissance—that people began creating more realistic-looking (and sometimes gory) crucifixes, which are crosses showing the crucified

Christ. Seven centuries later, overfamiliarity with the image of the cross has sometimes bred contempt, or at least indifference. Seeing mass-produced crucifixes on the dashboards of cars or the walls of Catholic hospitals and institutions has made many of us numb to the important message hidden there. But as Francis meditated on the cross, he saw a powerful, potent symbol of how life was to be lived in vital connection to both God and humanity.

In the vertical beam of the cross, which went from Jesus' head to his feet, Francis saw a symbol of God's love in action, of God reaching down to us from heaven. And in the horizontal beam, which supported Jesus' outstretched arms, Francis saw God's all-embracing love for humanity, and his desire to touch us with grace and healing.

Meditating further on the message of the cross, Francis knelt down on the ground and drew a cross in the dirt. Then he sent his friars off, two by two, into the four corners of the world, just as Jesus had sent his disciples into the world in pairs. The world is our cloister, said Francis, who urged his brothers out into the world as messengers of God, as servants of the world, and as evangelists for the teaching of Jesus.

Franciscans were among the first to take the message of Jesus to Asia and the New World, where they created a string of missions along the coast of California. The movement was also known for great preachers, such as St. Bernardino of Siena, St. John of Capistrano, and St. James of the Marches, who would preach to tens of thousands of people at a time. For these and other reasons, many people refer to Francis as the father of the modern missionary movement.

I look upon the world as my parish.—JOHN WESLEY

Evangelism conjures up a variety of images. And some people even argue that talking about religion and trying to persuade others to believe it is a rude, arrogant, and insensitive form of cultural imperialism.

Francis didn't see it that way. He understood evangelism as both a call of God and a social responsibility. It was a call of God, based on the words of Jesus in the Gospel of Matthew to: "Go and make disciples of all nations." It was a social responsibility because Francis believed he had been given a wonderful gift that held the answer to people's spiritual yearning. To keep it to himself would have been tantamount to keeping bread from someone dying of hunger.

The way the first Franciscan friars spread their message was certainly in contrast to the way others were promoting the Christian faith at that time. Remember the Crusades? For three centuries, hundreds of thousands of Christian crusaders crisscrossed Europe, forcing people to "convert" at the point of a sword. Contrast the violence of the Crusades with the gentle manner in which Francis sent out his friars on a crusade of real love: "As they go about the country, the friars are to take nothing with them for their journey. . . . They should not offer resistance to injury; if a man strikes them on the right cheek, they should turn the other cheek also towards him. If a man would take away their cloak, they should not grudge him their coat along with it. They should give to every man who asks, and if a man takes what is theirs, they should not ask him to restore it."

Before sending his friars throughout the world, Francis bent down and drew a cross on the ground. Perhaps he was thinking about an encounter he had with a crucifix years before.

One day while Francis was seeking God's guidance for his life, he stepped into the ruins of a small church called San Damiano. As Francis prayed and asked God for help, he heard the voice of Jesus speaking from a crucifix. "Francis, go, repair my house," said the voice. And Francis followed the order as best he knew how, carefully renovating the church using stones, mortar, muscles, and sweat.

Maybe, years later, as Francis drew that cross on the ground, he was beginning to see that Jesus had meant something entirely different. Perhaps the building Jesus wanted him to do didn't involve stones and mortar, but spiritual truth and hungry hearts. Maybe sending out friars into the four corners of the world was closer to what Jesus had really meant.

One thing's for sure, the message of love the friars took with them was embraced by many, the same way dry, parched ground soaks up the least bit of rain.

Preach always. If necessary, use words.—FRANCIS

Talk is cheap, but love is costly. When Francis and his friars went out into the world, they didn't practice a form of hit-and-run, kamikaze Christianity. They didn't just preach and run. They reached out to people and did what they could to serve. Thomas of Celano described Francis as "preaching everywhere the kingdom of God, and rendering his whole body a tongue, in order to edify his hearers by his example as well as by his words."

That's about as far as one can get from the highly publicized cases of contemporary preachers who live lives of wealth and sensuality while hypocritically telling their hearers to live godly lives. That's not the way it was with Francis. The message he taught was the message he lived. There was no disconnection between his words and his deeds, his public pronouncements and his private life.

The Franciscan approach of preaching and practicing the faith succeeded on a number of levels.

First, it was liberating for the friars because it allowed each individual to develop his own way to communicate the mercy of God. Like St. Anthony of Padua, some were good speakers, so preaching came naturally to them. Like Pacificus, a lute player, others were musicians who revealed their inspiration in their work. Like Blessed Giles of Assisi, some revealed the grace of God by serving others with humility, compassion, and love. All of these gifts could be used to demonstrate the reality of divine love.

Francis's approach also succeeded with the people who saw it in action. There was widespread skepticism about the institutional church during the Middle Ages, as in our own time. The medieval church was wealthy, powerful, corrupt, and hollow. Preaching the church's official doctrine would have gotten him nowhere without a simultaneous visible demonstration. Seeing faith in action helped people to believe. In this way, Francis made believers out of many.

I wish I could have heard Francis preach. I suspect his sermons were powerful, beautiful things. But for Francis, the measure of a good sermon wasn't based on rhetorical flourishes. It was based on results. Or as he put it, "There is no better sermon than the practice of the virtues."

Unfortunately, none of the saint's sermons has survived the centuries. But I can hear echoes of them in the lives of his followers around the world. And that's the way he would have liked it.

> *The free life was not, as some thought, a selfish life, for to be free was to be totally available.*
> —FATHER MURRAY BODO

I get nervous when people say they want to live at Little Portion Hermitage because of our community's solitude, isolation, and "paradise-like" character. It's true, our community is isolated and quiet. And for me it's a little paradise on earth. But those things aren't ends in themselves. Our purpose in turning down the noise and entanglements of life in the "real" world is to make ourselves available to God and others, which is frequently difficult and uncomfortable.

Community isn't some kind of Club Med for Christian mystics. It's not a religious theme park, where we can take a vacation from the pains and problems of the world. Instead, it's a spiritual incubator that helps us to grow and frees us up to serve. Francis taught that life is a beautiful, valuable thing. The way to lead a fulfilling life is to spend it in the service of others, not hiding away somewhere where our lives will be safe and protected.

"He was ready to spend himself," wrote Thomas of Celano. St. Bonaventure, who wrote about Francis years later, saw the same thing. "He wanted nothing more than to spend and be spent himself, in order to fulfill the duty of being compassionate towards others."

That's why Francis and his friars gave to the poor, cared for the lepers, suffered persecution, and sacrificed themselves for the benefit of others. It's a foundational characteristic of the Franciscan life that has marked the movement through the centuries.

I could cite dozens of examples from the past seven and a half centuries of Franciscan service. But two should suffice. During the Black Death of 1347, an estimated ten thousand friars lost their lives serving those afflicted with the fatal disease. And during the Holocaust of the Jews in twentieth-century Germany, St. Maximilian Kolbe and many other friars went to their deaths so Jews could live.

As Francis himself put it in his Rule for the brothers: "No matter where they are, the friars must always remember that they have given themselves up completely and handed over their whole selves to our Lord Jesus Christ, and so they should be prepared to expose themselves to every enemy, visible or invisible, for love of him."

I don't know about you, but when I listen to today's

church sermons, look at rack after rack of New Age self-help books, listen to popular spiritual leaders giving lectures, or hear human potential gurus hawking their tapes and products on cable TV, it seems that much contemporary spirituality is being sold the same way companies sell toothpaste, cars, and clothes. The emphasis is on the self. The come-ons seem to shout: "Buy God and you'll be healthier, wealthier, happier, and sexier."

Any spirituality that focuses on what it does for you alone is only telling a tiny part of the whole story. Spiritual growth leads directly to service. Spirituality that doesn't is stunted and incomplete.

> *If everyone would take only according to his needs and would leave the surplus to the needy, no one would be rich, no one poor, no one in misery.*
>
> —St. Basil

Theologians have debated for centuries about God's role in human affairs. Some ask how God could allow tragedies like crime, war, and famine. Others say the presence of such evils is proof that God doesn't exist at all. Francis was no theologian, but his answer to the eternal (and probably insoluble) dilemma of evil was both profound and practical, and it can be summarized in four simple words: We are God's hands.

It's not that God doesn't care about human tragedy. It's not that God is powerless to change things. God isn't absent without leave from the cosmos. Instead, God has placed tremendous responsibility in our hands. God is not some kind of divine puppet master, pulling our strings and determining all our actions. Instead, we were created free. Unfortunately, we often use our God-given freedom to cause harm and hatred. What is crime, but the abuse of some by others? What is war, but this abuse played out on a larger stage and spread across the globe? What is famine, but the imbalance of the world's resources, with some having nothing while others have plenty?

I recall one of our brothers describing a long prayer walk he took on the mountain paths surrounding our Little Portion Hermitage. The brother asked God, "Why do you allow poverty?" After a long silence, God answered the brother with a still, small voice that shook his soul: "Why do *you* allow poverty?"

God cares about our problems, and wants us to use the freedom we've been given to spread healing and love.

One day, someone asked Francis this seemingly simple question: Who are the true children of God? His answer was both direct and profound: "It is they who are the brides, the brothers and the mothers of our Lord Jesus Christ. A person is his bride when his faithful soul is united with Jesus Christ by the Holy Spirit; we are his brothers when we do the will of his Father who is in heaven; and we are mothers to him when we enthrone him in our hearts and souls by love with a pure and sincere conscience, and give him birth by doing good."

The concept that I give birth to God by doing good is a challenge to my soul. The truth that we incarnate Jesus when we serve others destroys the common distinction between "spiritual" work (praying, preaching, teaching) and other kinds of service (nursing the sick, feeding the hungry). It means that when members of our community help provide clothing to poor people in our area, God is mystically there in our midst, smiling upon that simple act of charity.

When I look at my own call to service, I realize God doesn't like me more when I play my guitar for thousands of people. I'm not superspiritual when I sing my songs about Jesus. But God beams with joy when I reach out my hand to someone who needs it. God is uniquely present in those moments of selfless service.

Faith without works is dead, said James the brother of Jesus. Spirituality that doesn't reach out beyond our selfish selves is like a body without hands. Love that isn't communicated through demonstrable acts is love unexpressed.

Whoever wants to become great among you must be your servant, and whoever wants to be first must be your slave.—Jesus

Like Jesus, Francis turned people's assumptions about greatness upside down. The Franciscan movement was incredibly more egalitarian than either the monasticism or the secular society of Francis's day. There were no upper and lower classes in Franciscan communities, and Francis did everything he could to soften such distinctions without totally doing away with the concept of leadership.

Those who supervise Franciscan communities aren't

called "prior," which means first, but "minister," which conveys a more pastoral feel. Francis described those ministers as "servants of the other friars." He condemned the pride that often accompanies positions of responsibility: "Those who are put in charge of others should be no prouder of their office than if they had been appointed to wash the feet of their [brothers]." He would not allow them to let their positions go to their heads: "All the friars without exception are forbidden to wield power or authority, particularly over one another." Ambition, which we generally regard as a good thing, meant that a person was disqualified from positions of leadership. And the responsibilities of office don't relieve one of the responsibilities to do manual labor and other mundane tasks.

From the perspective of the twentieth century, a time of widespread belief in democracy and the equality of all, it's hard for us to understand how radical Francis's approach was in the context of the socially stratified Middle Ages. Francis forbade his brothers from having anything to do with hierarchies or positions of leadership in the Roman Catholic Church (this was a hard-line position that his successors softened in the decades after his death but retained in spirit). Francis himself resigned from his position as Minister General of the order to live the life of an ordinary friar.

The biographies of the saint are overflowing with examples of his servant spirit and his teachings on the importance of downward mobility. But one of the most revealing snapshots of Francis's approach toward servant leadership is found in one brief sentence in the *Legend of*

Perugia that's easy to miss amid all the accounts of the saint's wonderful deeds. But there it is, hidden in a description of Francis's practice of traveling and preaching in churches: "He brought along a broom to clean the churches."

For Francis, preaching wasn't a chance to be a clerical celebrity or a Bible-expounding big shot. Rather, his visits to churches throughout Italy gave him an opportunity to serve in a disarmingly humble way, by sweeping dirt and dust out of houses of God.

Francis's unique approach to servant leadership is a daily inspiration to me as I try to do what's best for our community. His example—as well as numerous daily reminders of my own fallibility—keeps me from thinking more of myself than I should and falling to the temptation of bossing other people around.

> *Hell has three gates, lust, anger and greed.*
> —BHAGAVAD GITA

There are other compelling reasons that we are called to follow a life of service, made convincingly clear in a remarkable passage from the Bible. In the Gospel of Matthew, we find a description of Jesus at the end of time, sitting on a throne of judgment, and surrounded by everyone who ever lived.

First he looks at those on his right who are blessed by God. Why? Jesus tells us: "For I was hungry and you gave me something to eat, I was thirsty and you gave me something to drink, I was a stranger and you invited me in, I needed clothes and you clothed me, I was sick and you looked after me, I was in prison and you came to visit me."

The people are confused. They ask Jesus, when did we do these things? He answers them directly: "I tell you the truth, whatever you did for one of the least of these brothers of mine, you did for me."

Then Jesus speaks to those on his left, those who didn't feed the hungry, clothe the poor, care for the sick, or visit the prisoners. They're confused, too. But Jesus explains it all: "I tell you the truth, whatever you did not do for one of the least of these, you did not do for me."

Our eternal fate is determined by the millions of mundane daily decisions we make through the course of our lives. If we've lived in sync with God's will and served our brothers and sisters in need, we will inherit heaven. If we've lived lives of selfishness and self-centeredness, hell, whatever mysterious region that may be, is the place for us. But that doesn't mean those who serve others have to wait until after death to enjoy any benefits of their service. Instead, every time we help someone, we receive help from God. I know that's true for me.

For years I've worked with an organization named Mercy Corps, which is a Christian humanitarian organization working around the world. And in recent years, the Brothers and Sisters of Charity have begun our first missions to Central America, opening centers in Nicaragua and Honduras.

I've made numerous overseas trips where I tried to minister to the poor as best I could. But time after time, as I drag my worn, tired body back into some creaky bed for a brief night's sleep, I think about the people I met that day, the exchanges we had, and know in my heart that those people have loved me and touched me more than I could have ever helped them. Truly, these people are Jesus to me.

The necessity of service isn't something Francis or I made up. Rather, I think of it as one of the moral laws of the universe.

> *Remember that the Christian life is one of action; not of speech and daydreams.*—ST. VINCENT PALLOTTI

Who do you serve with your life, your time, your energy, your money? Do you have a concern for others? If so, how is that concern expressed?

I like to think that one of my songs, based on St. Teresa's Prayer, captures much of the essence of Francis's concept of service:

Christ has no body now but yours
No hands, no feet on earth but yours
Yours are the eyes through which he looks
Compassion on this world
Yours are the feet with which he walks to do good
Yours are the hands with which he blesses all the world.

Both Francis and Jesus prayed to God for direction, guidance, and a sense of their mission in life. You can do the same. Here's a prayer you can make your own:

"God, you made me. You love me. What would you have me do? Where would you have me go? Who would you have me serve? Show me how I can be your eyes of compassion, your heart of love, and your hands reaching out to this world. Amen."

There are almost an infinite number of ways you can serve. The needs are everywhere to be seen, both near and far. If God doesn't zap you with a telegram after you pray, you might do some exploring on your own:

✤ Give money to a worthy cause. We're living at a time when governments around the world are struggling to distribute limited or declining resources among an ever-expanding population of the needy and dispossessed. Increasingly, social observers are arguing that people like you and I need to shoulder more of the load and do more to help the hurting and heal the wounded.

You may mean well, but folks who are struggling to find a place to sleep or wondering where their next meal will come from aren't helped by your warm wishes. Open up your pockets and give to organizations and agencies that are providing critically needed assistance to society's needy.

✤ Go through your house from top to bottom, dig out things you don't use, and give them to someone who needs them. You may mean to lose a few extra pounds, but those shirts and pants that haven't fit you for years could keep someone warm tonight. That unusual lamp your relatives gave you untold Christmases ago has been collecting dust in the attic ever since, so why not let it bring light into someone else's home? Don't give others your worthless junk, but do pass on things that others could use. Perhaps you could even organize regular donation drives, where you collect goods from neighbors and friends and take them to a local facility that can clean them up and get them to people who could use them.

✦ Do you live near a church that runs a soup kitchen, clothing warehouse, or other ministry for poor people in your community? If so, you can work alongside these folks and learn from them about the needs all around you.

✦ I mentioned Mercy Corps, a Christian-based humanitarian group doing essential work around the world, as well as the missions of the Brothers and Sisters of Charity in Central America. Supporting efforts such as these may be more practical than trying to go on your own to foreign countries to serve. Consider sharing some of your resources with groups like these.

✦ On the other hand, maybe God is calling you to leave your comfort zone to serve those in need. Many groups also offer short-term trips that enable people to learn about other countries and see where they might be able to help. We at Little Portion would also be interested in hearing from you if you feel that's what God is calling you to do.

But on an even more basic level, perhaps you can think about ways you can begin being a servant to the people around you day after day. If you work, make a sincere effort to do your best for your bosses, and try to be a servant leader to those who report to you. Allow extra time in your day to buy a homeless person a sandwich or get gas for a stranded motorist. Listen and talk to others about their lives instead of yours.

If you are ready, willing, and available, opportunities to serve will come your way.

12

Peace

❦

Where there is hatred, let me sow love. —PEACE PRAYER OF ST. FRANCIS

MUCH OF MY LIFE IS SPENT in relative quiet and serenity at the Little Portion Hermitage, the community where I and others attempt to live according to the teachings of Francis. But the rest of my life is spent in places like Los Angeles, New York, Nashville, and Chicago, performing and teaching, meeting with people involved in the music and publishing industries, and spending a seeming eternity in cars on crowded highways and byways. Every city has wonderful people, but each also has its dreaded drives. My least favorite place to drive is on the crowded web of concrete and asphalt encircling Los Angeles, where going a few miles can take a few hours.

I remember one hot and congested day when the usually molasses-like flow of vehicles hardened into stone. The red-faced drivers parked all around me vented their frustration with a discordant symphony of horns and yells and a vigorous display of hand gestures which, at least to this brother, didn't appear to be peace signs.

Finally focusing my attention on the car that had been in front of me for the past ninety minutes, I noticed a bumper sticker that said VISUALIZE WORLD PEACE.

Having nowhere to go and nothing better to do, I gave it a try. I imagined what peace would look like if it suddenly broke out on the stretch of highway where I and hundreds of others were stranded. I pictured people talking and joking together instead of yelling and gesturing, praying for people who may have been involved in an accident ahead instead of fuming and stressing over their inconvenience.

Then, I started visualizing what would happen if peace spread out from my tiny spot in concentric circles. What if angels of brotherly love wrapped their wings around Los Angeles, a city where tensions seem to simmer under the surface until they erupt in televised anger and violence? What if peace covered North and South America, where differences of race, class, religion, and culture often divide neighbor from neighbor? What if peace enveloped the world, eliminating warfare, ethnic cleansing, and . . .

Suddenly I was jarred out of my reverie by the ear-shattering sound of one horn blaring. The driver behind me was letting me know that a three-foot space had opened up between me and the VISUALIZE WORLD PEACE bumper sticker and encouraging me to move along. My minimeditation hadn't done much to calm his nerves, and as I watched television newscasts over the next few days, it became clear that the world wasn't much more peaceful, either.

Bringing peace to the world—or to my little corner of it—is going to take more than visualization. And the life and lessons of Francis give us a practical and spiritually proven plan for putting peace into action.

War is hell.—WILLIAM TECUMSEH SHERMAN

Francis was known as a man of peace, and in the seven centuries since his death, the Franciscan movement has been known for building bridges of communication, understanding, and cooperation between warring people, groups, and nations.

It's surprising, then, to see that this man of peace was born into a period of incredible turbulence, strife, violence, and warfare. In his lifetime, Europe's once-unshakable feudal system was breaking apart under the assaults of hundreds of small-scale peasant revolts. And Italy's provinces and cities were ensnared in an ongoing strife that led to a near-continual state of war.

During his youth, Francis watched as his own town of Assisi was wracked by a civil war, during which the castles belonging to the town's feudal nobles were destroyed, as well as a long-running conflict with the nearby town of Perugia. Shortly after Francis's twentieth birthday, the conflict with Perugia erupted into outright war. Inspired by patriotism and youthful pride, Francis enlisted, but before he saw battle he was captured and put in prison, where he languished for nearly a year.

Two years later, Francis set out again for war, this time

in a papal army bound for the Crusades. But during this assault he was captured by Jesus, the Prince of Peace. On his way to battle, Francis was stopped dead in his tracks by a vision from God. He tried to understand the vision, but his experience was a little like someone trying to listen to a broadcast on a malfunctioning radio. Instead of receiving a complete program for his life, Francis only got bits and pieces of a complex puzzle, which he spent most of the next year desperately trying to unscramble. In the process, he came to a deep faith in God, gave himself to living the life that Jesus led, and turned from the pursuit of warfare to the practice of peace.

Today, millions of people around the world carry a copy of the St. Francis Peace Prayer in their wallets, tape it to their computers at work, or hang it on the walls of their homes. Although no one's sure Francis himself actually wrote the prayer, it embodies his commitment to peace and his willingness to give of himself to make it a living reality:

Lord, make me an instrument of your peace;
where there is hatred, let me sow love;
where there is injury, pardon;
where there is doubt, faith;
where there is despair, hope;
where there is darkness, light;
and where there is sadness, joy.
Grant that I may not so much seek to be consoled
    as to console;

to be understood as to understand;
to be loved as to love;
for it is in giving that we receive;
it is in pardoning that we are pardoned;
and it is in dying that we are born to eternal life.

We have been called to heal wounds, to unite what has fallen apart, and to bring home those who have lost their way.—FRANCIS

Francis was born centuries too early to receive the Nobel Peace Prize, but he would have been a shoo-in for the award if nominated today, for his life was a tireless exercise in waging peace. During his brief forty-five years, Francis lived like some kind of medieval combination of Jimmy Carter and Mother Teresa, popping up in an incredible number of his world's hot spots, putting himself in continual danger, reaching out to unite bitter foes, and greeting people with a simple blessing—"God give you peace"—the peace which he said God had given him.

Francis also said God revealed something else to him: that spiritual forces were largely responsible for the ongoing warfare in the city of Arezzo, one of the first places where Francis waged peace. Staying in a hospital on the outskirts of the city, Francis became convinced demons were egging the citizens on to war. So he dispatched Brother Sylvester to the town to order the devils to leave the city. The demons departed and the people settled their differences.

Later, Francis and some of the friars were approaching the city of Siena, where fighting had erupted, resulting in the death of two citizens. Francis entered the city where, according to the *Little Flowers*, he "preached to those men in such a beautiful and holy way that he brought all of them back to peace and great unity and harmony."

A year before his death, an aged and sickly Francis used his art to heal an ugly rift between church and state in his own hometown. No one's sure how the tiff began, but the town's bishop excommunicated the governor, who then ordered all citizens to have no further contact with the bishop. These two respected pillars of the community continued to act like two impetuous schoolchildren, throwing the whole town into confusion.

Summoning all his creative energies, Francis composed a new final stanza to his recently completed "The Canticle of Brother Sun":

> All praise be yours, my Lord,
> Through those who grant pardon for love of you;
> Through those who endure sickness and trial.
> Happy those who endure in peace;
> By you, Most High, they will be crowned.

Too weak to do so himself, Francis instructed his friars to contact the governor and urge him to go to the bishop's house, where both men would hear the "world premiere" of his new verse. "I have confidence that the Lord will put humility and peace in their hearts and that they will return to their former friendship and affection," said Francis.

A stony silence filled the cloister of the bishop's palace, but as soon as the friars began singing, the two men's hard hearts melted. "I forgive the lord bishop whom I ought to recognize as my master," vowed the governor. The bishop responded in kind: "My office demands humility of me, but by nature I am quick to anger; you must forgive me!" The friar who recorded the event would have made a successful television script-writer, noting a happily-ever-after postscript: "With much tenderness and affection, both locked arms and embraced each other."

Francis wouldn't have won the Nobel Peace Prize merely for refereeing a few regional squabbles. But the judges might have been swayed in his favor by this his-toric fact: Francis demilitarized Europe. When Francis wrote the Rule for his Third Order, or "secular" Francis-cans, he included this radical pledge: "They are not to take up lethal weapons, or beat them about, against anybody."

Slowly but surely, as Francis's ragtag movement grew from a handful of friars to a movement of hun-dreds of thousands, every country of Europe was infil-trated by the saint's agents of peace. A Franciscan peace movement swept across the globe, leading people to lay down their weapons and their disputes, and dealing a final death blow to the militaristic feudal system.

Today, the Franciscans still wage peace around the world. Many contemporary Franciscans are adding a fourth vow of nonviolence to the traditional Franciscan vows of poverty, chastity, and obedience; and they're seeking practical ways to apply Jesus' injunction to "turn the other cheek."

For this and for other accomplishments in the promotion of peace, I recognize Francis of Assisi, who continually practiced and preached peace. Or in the words of one who knew him: "Throughout his discourse he spoke of putting an end to hatreds."

> *First keep peace within yourself, then you can also bring peace to others.*—THOMAS À KEMPIS

Francis was a man of peace during a time of war. He was a builder of bridges in an age when people were tearing down castles and anything else that symbolized feudal authority. But most amazing of all, Francis was a man who showed deep respect for Muslims at the height of the mother of all holy wars—the Crusades.

Launched in 1095, the Crusades were an effort to rescue Jerusalem from Muslim invaders, but by the time they ended three centuries later, the Crusades had evolved into a continent-wide series of campaigns and battles against not only Muslims but also pagans, heretics, and other "enemies of Christ."

Official church documents referred to disciples of Islam as "dogs" and "wicked people," and crusading soldiers treated them as such. One Arab chronicler described the gory aftermath of the Battle of Hattin in 1187 as a field of "severed heads, eyes dulled or gouged out, bodies covered with dust, dismembered limbs, severed arms, split bones . . . feet hanging by a thread from legs, bodies cut in two, torn lips, smashed foreheads."

Into the midst of this horror and hatred walked Francis. After numerous efforts to talk to Muslim leaders had been foiled, he crossed enemy lines during the Fifth Crusade near Damietta, Egypt, risking his life in the hopes that he could have a personal audience with Melek el-Khamil, the sultan of Babylon, whom he hoped to convert to Christianity—not with weapons but with words. As G. K. Chesterton put it, Francis followed this simple maxim: "It is better to create Christians than to destroy Moslems."

The mission to convert the sultan was unsuccessful. But though he remained a committed Muslim, he did develop an affection for Francis—the kind of affection that reportedly led him to remark that if there were more Christians like Francis, he'd consider becoming one.

One can hear people echo such sentiments today when they complain about the poor treatment they've received from a religious leader or institution, when they find that yet another priest or minister has been caught in sexual infidelities or financial misdeeds, or when they hear a conservative religious activist lashing out at a convenient scapegoat.

By setting out on a mission of persuasion at a time when the majority of Christian Europe was involved in a war of compulsion, Francis showed the strength and courage required of those who try to wage peace. By evangelizing through word and deed rather than by sword and cudgel, he gave a living of example of Christianity in action, and sowed the seeds of religious liberty and toleration.

Give to every other human being every right that you claim yourself.—ROBERT G. INGERSOLL

Over the centuries, Francis's example of communicating the Gospel in a loving, living way has inspired millions: leading some to spread a spiritual message through the mass media; encouraging others to use the arts and their God-given creativity; and giving others the courage to cross enemy lines for the cause of peace. Unlike Francis, many of these friars died in the process, showing through their death that peace is a costly proposition.

The pages of Franciscan history are full of examples of selfless love in action. Third Order Franciscan Ramón Llull (anglicized Raymond Lully, 1235–1316) took a page out of Francis's own life when he criticized the Crusades and advocated a "peaceful crusade" to the Muslims. Instead of loading up on weapons, Llull filled his mind with Middle Eastern knowledge, spending nine years learning the Arabic language and studying the intricacies of Muslim philosophy and theology. He learned to debate with Muslim scholars, and wrote books on spirituality as well as volumes of mystical poetry.

But he didn't try to force conversions by beating people over the head. Instead, he showed respect for Muslim people, their culture, and their religion.

Llull found a bond of common human respect underneath the theological differences. He wished with all his heart that Muslims would convert to Christianity and didn't paper over real and significant disagreements between Christians and Muslims about the nature of God and the purpose of life. But he didn't try to force conversions by beating people over the head. Instead, he showed respect for Muslim people, their culture, and their religion. He confronted the differences between two cultures head-on, but he went beyond the differences to a respect based on one thing they all had in common: They were all made in God's image and deserving of respect.

If only more people followed this example; unfortunately, that's not the case. Over the course of human history, horrible things have been done in the name of God. But that doesn't mean sharing one's deepest beliefs and values with another has to be disrespectful. In fact, both Islam and Christianity are essentially evangelistic faiths and adherents of both religions are urged to spread their respective faith. But Francis shows us what it means to share one's faith without disrespecting the faith of another, and this is a lesson that could help many contemporary fundamentalists, both Bible-thumpers and Koran-thumpers. This is a lesson we can apply to all kinds of conflicts, whether they be about religion, or other hot topics like politics, the weather, or sports.

"Proclaim the word of God openly," wrote Francis in a section of his Rule dealing with evangelism to the Muslims. But that bold proclamation was balanced with his injunction "to avoid quarrels or disputes and be subject to every human creature for God's sake." In Francis's age of intense religious rivalry and warfare, this was uncommonly good wisdom. It's still good advice today, when religious fundamentalism is experiencing a resurgence around the globe.

All you need is love.—THE BEATLES

"Better Find Jesus" was a song that my early country-rock group Mason Proffit recorded on its 1972 album, *Rockfish Crossing*. The chorus included these lines, which were an indictment of the student antiwar movement:

> Talkin' 'bout the world
> And how it's wrong and right
> You're screamin' for peace
> And then you're ready to fight
> Throwin' a brick in the name of love
> Talkin' but you never settle anything.

For myself and for many other musicians singing at that time, we sincerely believed that our songs about peace could not only help end the Vietnam War but also bring about a universal period of love, or "Age of Aquarius." This idealism was reflected in other songs like the Beatles' "All You Need Is Love" and George Harrison's "Give Me Love (Give Me Peace on Earth)."

Such songs helped inspire a worldwide peace movement, part of which was based on the principles of nonviolence used by Gandhi in India and by Martin Luther King Jr. in the American civil rights movement.

But I and many others watched in shock and revulsion as members of the peace movement began using the techniques of war to fight for peace. Increasingly, some activists utilized decidedly nonpeaceful means to pursue their agenda. Bombings, killings, violent demonstrations, and assorted terrorist tactics were commonplace, and all were excused as being essential for the cause. Those who defended such tactics said they were justified by their results: The war in Vietnam ended, and

American troops came home. But the aftermath of the peace movement was a legacy of pain, suspicion, mistrust, and generational division that still affects much of the Western world.

Francis shows us a far more revolutionary approach. The man who prayed, "Lord, where there is hatred, let me sow love," teaches us that those who want peace must first possess it in their hearts and then give birth to it in the world.

The lessons of Francis can be applied today to a conflict some have labeled a "culture war" over moral principles. One can hear plenty of warfare rhetoric on complex and controversial issues like abortion and homosexuality, as activists on both sides talk about allies and enemies, strategies and combat, victory and defeat. Their confrontations are full of people screaming through bullhorns, waving flags and banners, and spreading untruth and division through propaganda that distorts the other side's actions and intentions. Sometimes, the language of culture war translates into real acts of violence and killing, such as bombings and shootings, revealing that culture war and military war both share common elements such as anger and hatred.

But in the midst of the fiery words and angry rhetoric, some committed proponents are following Francis's example and crossing "enemy" lines. For example, some Christians work with women who are dealing with the complications of unplanned or unwanted pregnancies, helping them think through the options they face. These humble servants demonstrate love, even if women make choices they don't agree with. Their love isn't conditional.

It isn't based on whether people make the "right" choices; it's based on God's love for us. Elsewhere, agents of peace work as volunteers in AIDS hospices, where they provide physical, emotional, and spiritual comfort to those dying of this terrible illness, despite being criticized by conservative Christians for fraternizing with the "enemy" and labeled as suspicious by some because of their deep faith.

Whether one is in the midst of a culture war, where fighting involves words and issues, or a full-scale military conflagration with bullets and bombs, there's always a need for peacemakers who will cross enemy lines, show respect and love, and proclaim the mercy of God.

> *If you love peace, then hate injustice, hate tyranny, hate greed—but hate these things inside yourself, not in another.*—GANDHI

Are you an agent of peace or an accomplice to war? Do your activities in the world sow peace and love or bitterness and hate? Are you crossing enemy lines to extend a hand of love and mercy to people who are different from you or who disagree with you, or are you an angry combatant who is suspicious and mistrustful of "them"?

Or, to put it another way, what fills your heart: peace or turmoil? Grace or anger? What if we performed open-heart surgery on you right now? What would we find? Would your exam reveal a warm heart full of compassion and mercy? Or would it find a cold heart, chained by ancient resentments and hostilities and corroded by the acid of bitterness?

Francis was a loving doctor who constantly warned his

friars against illnesses of the heart: "As you preach peace by word, so you should also possess peace, and super-abundant peace in your hearts." It may sound trite or sophomoric, but unless we have peace in our hearts we can't be agents of peace in the world.

Stop and listen to your heart. What do you hear? If you're full of anger and bitterness, the best prescription is forgiveness. Maybe someone hurt you long ago, and that hurt has festered and hardened. Release it by forgiving the one who injured you. That doesn't mean you're saying what's wrong is right. And it doesn't mean you become vulnerable to further injury. Quite the contrary, you become vulnerable to love and mercy, which are two prerequisites for sowing peace in the world.

Ask God to give you the gift of his peace. Invite God to reveal to you ways in which you may be unknowingly creating havoc and discord. Ask for the strength to forgive and love, which require more energy and spiritual maturity than holding grudges and acting out of anger.

Blessed are the peacemakers, for they will be called sons of God.—JESUS

If your heart is relatively free of mistrust and anger, or even if you're already in the process of undergoing a change of heart, there are plenty of practical steps you can take toward waging peace in the world.

First, consciously practice goodness, purity, and non-resistance, no matter what others do to you. Too many would-be peacemakers start out with good intentions, but they change course and react with anger when they are attacked or criticized. Responding to evil with good and answering hate with love is a powerful thing, as Francis pointed out: "When we hear or see people speaking or doing evil or blaspheming God, we must say and do good, praising God, who is blessed forever." Maybe there are people in your life who try to hurt and harass you. Don't give in to them, but don't give up on them either. When they throw flaming darts of angry words or harsh actions at you, send them a loving heart.

Also, be ready to respond in a conciliatory way when you find yourself in the middle of an argument or conflict. Let's face it, some battles can't be won. And it's a sure thing that some people are never going to be persuaded to your point of view, no matter how right you are or how eloquently or passionately you drive home your point. Instead of fighting to the bitter end, agree to disagree. That doesn't mean you're compromising your values or giving in. It just means that your commitment to mutual respect, civility, and keeping bridges of communication open is more important than scoring a few points in a petty argument.

And if you find yourself in a tense situation where you're surrounded by hot tempers and hurt feelings, ask God to give you his peace. Calm your heart, still your mind, and begin breathing slowly as you pray for peace. Make each breath a prayer. As you inhale and exhale, meditate on the grace and love of God. When I do that, I find that my heart rate slows down and I am filled with an inner calm that allows me to be a instrument of God's peace in the world. This may seem like a small thing, but I believe if more people practiced peace, the world would see less violence and warfare.

Join with me. Volunteer for service in the forces of love. Wage peace.

13

Prayer

Let us be ashamed to be caught up by worthless imaginings, for at the time of prayer we speak to the great King.

—FRANCIS

THIS MAY SEEM STRANGE TO SOME people, but I don't get nervous when I play my music for a crowd of twenty thousand in a coliseum, but set me down with my guitar at a wedding and I turn to jelly. Just about every time this "professional" provides a special song or instrumental music at a friend's wedding, I feel my knees going weak, a lump forming in my throat, and my mouth growing dry.

The reason I lose my composure at weddings is because of a deep feeling that I'm walking on holy ground. The mystical union of a man and a wife, combined with the sounds and sights of laughter and tears, children, family, friends, and well-wishers, fills me with an overwhelming sense of the sacred.

Many religious traditions honor marriage as a sacrament, in part because weddings are moving and mysterious occasions where something happening here on earth reaches out across the universe to the heart of God. In marriage, the material meets the mystical, flesh and blood mix with spirit and soul.

For me, the ceremony of marriage is also a metaphor for prayer. Now I know that when many people think of prayer, they picture something formal, ritualistic, or even dead. They recall a stony benediction a priest once gave at a church service, a pious platitude recited before a large banquet, or a droning monologue that sounds more like a sermon than a prayer. Or, they think of those desperate pleadings for the universe to change its course, like the plea a quarterback whispers while he throws a blind pass into the end zone, or like the hope an ill-prepared student expresses right before he's about to get an F on a class final.

In reality, prayer is a mystical union between God and us. It's a form of communication that makes our relationship to God personal and vital. It's not a cold, impersonal ritual, but a warm and loving embrace between the God of the universe and a humble, hungry soul.

Francis didn't spell out an elaborate plan for how and when to pray. In fact, most people who follow in the footsteps of Francis believe the saint was so wrapped up actually praying, preaching, and serving that he didn't have the time or inclination to merely talk about prayer. But his example and his few teachings on the subject and the mystical nature of the movement he founded show us how prayer can be our doorway to the loving heart of God and our lifeline to a moment-by-moment spiritual vitality that can energize and transform our lives.

Everything that one turns in the direction of God is a prayer.—ST. IGNATIUS LOYOLA

Sometimes, as I'm singing at a wedding, I look at the two people who are walking down the aisle, and I wonder how much they really know about each other. She may not know everything there is to know about him, such as his tendency to wear the same pair of sweat socks for what seems like weeks at a time, along with his other idiosyncrasies and habits. And he may not know everything there is to know about her, such as her utter revulsion for smelly sweat socks, as well as other passions and preferences. But as anyone who's been married for any time at all can tell you, a lifetime isn't long enough to know everything about a partner.

Thankfully, getting married doesn't require that two partners *know everything* there is to know about each other. There's no crash quiz given, with people who get a failing grade being prohibited from wedding. But success at marriage does require that two partners *know* each other, that they have achieved some level of interpersonal intimacy, and that the two people getting married aren't total strangers. The same goes for friendship. I don't have to have exhaustive knowledge about you, your history, your values, and your activities to be your friend. But I do have to know you, and allow myself to be known by you.

The same really goes for just about anything. You may be able to build a boat and lecture about nautical history, but if you've never set sail in the water I'll say you don't know boating. You might be able to tell me incredibly detailed biographical information about

Beethoven, and explain how he wrote his numerous symphonies, concertos, and overtures. But if you've never wept while listening to his seventh symphony, I'll say you haven't begun to know the man and his work.

There's a world of difference between *knowing about* something and actually *knowing* something. One is head knowledge, and the other is heart knowledge, and better still is intuition. There's no comparing cold, intellectual facts you have gathered about someone to intimate, life-changing experiences you have gone through with someone.

This simple difference between *knowing about* and *knowing* is a fundamental part of the way Francis related to God. Francis's goal in life wasn't to be Italy's most respected religious scholar, reciting theological theorems propounding doctrinal dogmas. He wanted to be deeply and madly in love with God. And that's what he would want for you and me, too.

The more we love God, the more we will want to love him.—St. Joaquina

I've read hundreds of books about God by everybody from Christian friars to Buddhist monks. Surprisingly, when people from diverse faiths talk about prayer, they all sound much alike. And while all of these books have helped me understand something more about the spiritual life, if I had been a Franciscan during Francis's brief lifetime, I probably would have spent less time reading and more time praying. That's because Francis had a deep distrust of book knowledge.

"He prayed more than he studied," wrote one biographer. Another wrote that the saint's theology didn't come from reading books about God, but "that he had been taught by the Holy Spirit without the aid of man," and "the secrets of divine wisdom were made known to him." When Brother John of Stracchia, who was in charge of the friary in Bologna, founded a house of religious studies, Francis went to John and criticized him: "You want to destroy my Order! For I want my friars to pray more than to read, according to the example of my Lord Jesus Christ."

Another time, Francis lectured the brothers on the dangers of intellectual arrogance: "There are many brothers who day and night put all their energy and all their attention into the pursuit of knowledge, thereby abandoning prayer and their holy vocation. And when they have preached to a few men or to the people, and learn that certain ones were edified or converted . . . they are puffed up and pride themselves on the results."

Don't get me wrong. Francis wasn't a numskull, and the Franciscan movement isn't anti-intellectual. In fact, renowned poets like Dante and philosophers like John Duns Scotus became Franciscans with no noticeable harm to their minds and no significant diminishment of their creative output. It's just that Francis knew that the world (and maybe even the church) is full of people who mistake knowing things about God for actually knowing God. And he wasn't about to let the same thing happen in his movement.

Today, scientific evidence is mounting in support of the practical benefits of prayer. Study after study has shown that people who pray are happier, healthier, and nicer to be around. Francis knew all this centuries before the guys in white lab coats found a way to prove it. He didn't want his followers to be full of learning but empty of life. He wanted his movement to be populated by people who knew God intimately and exhibited God's love and energy in their lives and in their relationship to the world.

> *Silence is a gift of God, to let us speak more intimately with God.*—St. Vincent Pallotti

If prayer can be compared to marriage, then the process of learning how to pray can be compared to the process of falling in love. Franciscan friar Ramón Llull called his manual on prayer *The Book of the Lover and the Beloved,* a title which I borrowed for my own book on Franciscan prayer, *The Lover and the Beloved.*

Many of my friends are shocked the first time they hear prayer being described in romantic terms. For them, there's something improper or even slightly sacrilegious about comparing prayer, a thing so lofty and spiritual, to love. But it didn't bother Francis or other saints. They could think of no better way to describe the union between God and humans. The Bible often describes God as a lover who desires to know us and be known by us, as a partner who wants total intimacy with us in every aspect of our lives, and as a parent who has many spiritual offspring.

God's love for us is pure, passionate, selfless, and relentless. It's a love that allows us the freedom to accept it or reject it, for God would never manipulate or overrule our wills. But if we accept that love, it brings ecstasy and rapture. Trying to contain God's overwhelming love for us is like trying to hold the ocean in a thimble.

> *Prayer is conversation with God.*
> —St. Clement of Alexandria

The beginnings of our prayer relationship with God can be compared to the early stages of romance. For some mysterious reason, a spark occurs between a man and a woman, and they are drawn to each other in a way that defies explanation. As they grow closer, they learn more about one another by opening their hearts, their speech revealing the inner qualities of each person. As words, thoughts, and feelings are shared, their inner selves are revealed. Our intimacy with God develops the same way—through words—though at first it seems we have to do most of the talking, revealing our inner selves to God through our requests, our confessions, and our vulnerability.

We can begin to learn more about God through words already there for us in the Scriptures, which are not just a series of laws and doctrines, but a window into God's heart. Study and meditation of God's revelation is the best way to grow in knowledge and understanding.

We can also learn by reading the thoughts of those saints who have known, followed, and walked with God. We can learn much from creation as well and from taking the time to hear the voice of God in nature through prayer walks and meditation. All creation bears the traces of the Creator and will lead the spiritually sensitive seeker back to God.

But it doesn't end there. In romance, the process of learning and growing closer to each other is soon complemented by touch. The mystical union between God and us happens in much the same way. After a period of time in which we have come to know more about God through study, meditation, and the speaking of words, we begin to experience God through the touch of mystical union. In *Franciscan Mysticism* Brother Boniface Maes writes, "The grace of God sometimes overflows like a river and invades the emotional power of the soul . . . there follows spiritual intoxication, which is a breaking out of overwhelming tenderness and delicious intimacies greater than the heart can desire or contain."

This kind of mystical contemplation is beyond anything we can define or describe, just as it's impossible to describe the euphoria of sexual union. It's beyond logic, hidden in the realm of mystery and paradox. It can't be manipulated, and we can't manufacture it on command. We can only set the stage and wait for it to happen, by God's grace.

I have felt this touch of God's spirit many times when walking in the woods. The first time was at the Trappist monastery of Gethsemani in Kentucky. I found myself bounding down secluded paths, singing loud praises to God, and inviting all of creation to join in with me. I sang with the birds. I sang with the spring flowers. I do not remember the songs I sang, but I am sure God enjoyed them as my greatest works of art.

> *Let us learn to cast our hearts into God.*
>
> —St. Bernard

Francis jealously guarded his time alone with God, much the way a lover protects shared moments with a partner. Biographies of the saint are brimming over with colorful descriptions of the lengths to which Francis would go to be alone in God's presence, the way this deep spiritual intimacy affected his entire life.

While visiting a friend near the Lake of Perugia, Francis felt an inner nudging to go away and be alone with God. He asked his friend to drop him off on a solitary island in the lake, pleaded with him not to reveal the location to anyone, and requested that the friend pick him up in forty days. Left on the island, which had no buildings, Francis found a dense thicket of thorn bushes and small trees, and built a small shelter in the middle of the thicket. Then he got down to business: "And he began to pray and contemplate heavenly things in that place."

Because Francis realized that it wouldn't always be practical for him and his followers to disappear into the wilderness for weeks at a time, he founded two dozen hermitages during his life, creating havens for intense spiritual intimacy all over the Italian countryside. But while throughout Christian history, people have gone to great lengths to create monasteries and hermitages in out-of-the-way places, that's not the approach Francis took. He founded his houses of prayer within easy walking distance of nearby cities so his friars could practice the balancing act between solitary intimacy with God and selfless service to God's people.

For Francis, solitude and service were two sides of the same coin. His followers weren't detached from the world like island-dwelling monks, nor were they totally wrapped up in the world like full-service social workers. Francis and his friars were torn between being alone with

God and being in the midst of the throngs. But it was clear to Francis that it was the time alone with God that made the periods of service meaningful and productive.

As important as those times of spiritual intimacy with God were to Francis, in the end the experience was impossible to describe, as one biographer wrote: "Francis was often suspended in such sweetness of contemplation that, caught up out of himself, he could not reveal what he had experienced because it went beyond all human comprehension."

> *In God alone there is primordial and true delight, and in all our delights it is this delight that we are seeking.*—ST. BONAVENTURE

Francis did his best to get away and be alone with God, but his friars frequently followed him, observing him from a safe distance the same way students might follow a beloved teacher to see what he's like once he's outside the classroom.

To just about nobody's surprise, they discovered that the private Francis was much the same as the public Francis, except that when the saint was alone in prayer, he would give free rein to his emotions: laughing one minute and crying the next, singing mystical love songs in French at the top of his lungs one instant, and praying in hushed silence the next. Francis had two good reasons to keep these displays to himself. For one, they were part of his private communication with his divine lover. For another, such behavior would only give ammunition to those who claimed the saint was unstable.

At times, the friars' fantastical descriptions of the

things they saw when Francis prayed sound more like scripts for *The X-Files* than descriptions of a saint at prayer. One observer described Francis as some kind of shimmering, hovering, spinning UFO. Another thought he resembled a flame-throwing volcano. Yet another friar saw something on the order of the aurora borealis in the skies surrounding the saint's spiritual retreat. And another recorded that the hills and valleys around Francis's hermitage at Mount La Verna were lit by flames so bright that some travelers staying in nearby inns thought the sun had risen and got out of bed to resume their journeys.

One friar who kept watch over a praying Francis reported how "a most splendid fiery chariot entered through the door of the house and turned around two or three times here and there inside the house; a huge globe of light rested above it, much like the sun, and it lit up the night." Such descriptions may seem more appropriate to a psychedelic experience, but I can assure you that Francis and his friars weren't stoned on anything but the reality of God in their midst.

Near the end of his life, Francis had another one of his legendary prayer experiences, but this time the accompanying miracles weren't projected into the sky like some laser light show, but etched on the saint's own frail body. By the time Francis was forty-three, his infirmities kept him from ministering in public as much as he would like, which meant he got to spend more time alone with God. As the early biographies unanimously report, during one of these periods of prayer, Francis was meditating on Christ's Passion—his brutal death on the cross—and praying that his life would imitate the life of

Jesus in every way when he was visited by God in a unique and powerful way. As he prayed, an angel visited the saint and left on his hands, feet, and side the same wounds Christ received on the cross.

Francis is not the only person to have received such marks, called stigmata, over the centuries. Hundreds of saints and mystics have claimed to have experienced similar visitations, resulting in wounds that were either visible or invisible, temporary or permanent. Interestingly, the Catholic Church has never defined the precise origin of these events, leaving their cause open to a variety of physical, psychological and spiritual interpretations. And the church has only very rarely accepted such reports as authentic, including among this small number the case of Francis, who bore the scars until his death.

> *If it is possible, may this cup be taken from me. Yet not as I will, but as you will.*—JESUS

When I compare Francis's life to the life of Jesus, one striking similarity grabs me: Both drew strength from intense periods of spiritual isolation prior to engaging in tireless and selfless work in the world. For these two spiritual teachers, prayer wasn't a private treasure designed to give them spiritual goose bumps or make them happier, healthier, and wealthier. Prayer was a method of allowing God to recharge their spiritual batteries for loving others.

As I read through the Gospels, I see how Jesus went to secret and lonely spots to meditate and pray before encountering some of the pivotal moments in his ministry, such as his temptations by Satan, his sending of the twelve apostles to spread the Word, his transfiguration, his last supper with his disciples, and his crucifixion. Likewise, his biographers show that Francis was frequently lost in prayer before he preached, before his many divine visions, before writing the Rules for the first Franciscan communities, and before crucial periods of decision in the life of his movement.

The prayers Jesus and Francis said weren't like my own often selfish, petty prayers, many of which ask God to help me do some task or get some benefit. No, theirs were prayers of searching, submission, and dependence. They didn't go to God with a long shopping list of all the goodies they wanted. They went to God straining to hear that still, small voice, seeking to understand what God wanted them to do, and when, and where!

We shouldn't think of prayer as if it's the "Get Out of Jail Free" card, only to be used in case of dire emergencies. Or as our chance to tell God about all the great stuff we would do if only we got the right job, car, or house. Pray with the listening attentiveness you would show to someone you deeply love and desperately want to please. Instead of going to God with an agenda, pray with open hands, heart, and mind.

More things are wrought by prayer
Than this world dreams of.
       —Alfred, Lord Tennyson

There's so much more I could say about prayer, but ultimately, it's a complex mystery that's impossible to describe. That's particularly true of something known as "contemplative prayer," a form of communion with God that saints have described as the highest form of prayer one can know.

Contemplative prayer is beyond words, beyond ideas, beyond emotion, and beyond form. One saint described it as a breakthrough to the infinite. Another talked about how contemplative prayer transcends distinctions between body and soul, transporting our spiritual essence to the presence of God. Perhaps St. Bonaventure put it best: "If you wish to know how such things come about, consult grace, not doctrine; desire, not understanding; prayerful groaning, not studious reading; God, not man."

I believe Francis would be disappointed if this chapter were merely a theoretical discourse. Here I am, like some beach-bound swim instructor describing the breast stroke. Meanwhile, Francis has stripped off his robe and jumped into the ocean, where he waves his hands and hollers, "Come on in! The water's fine!" So with that in mind, allow me to quit pontificating and begin sharing with you some of the lessons in prayer I have learned over the years.

✤ Make the time and find a place. Any relationship requires time to cultivate it, including your relationship with God. One of the best things about living here at the Little Portion Hermitage is that our lives are scheduled around periods of prayer and meditation in our chapel. That way, the really important things aren't squeezed out of our lives by things that are less important. You need to do the same. Make a time and a place for prayer in your life. Schedule regular periods when you can pray to God every day. Set aside a place where you can pray comfortably and without distraction. And consider occasions when you can spend even more time alone with God, such as special times of prayer once a week, monthly retreats, or annual visits to a nearby monastery or prayer center.

✤ Follow others' examples. Don't try to reinvent the wheel, but take tips from others who have learned the discipline of prayer. In chapter 6 of Matthew, Jesus tells his disciples how to pray in a passage we refer to as the Lord's Prayer. Learn this prayer, practice it, and use it as a jumping-off point for your own prayers. The psalms are another excellent manual. Start with the meditation in Psalm 1, and read through a different psalm every day as you pray. One of the oldest and simplest prayers in the Christian tradition is The Jesus Prayer:

> Lord Jesus Christ, son of God,
> Have mercy on me, a sinner.

This prayer has been used for centuries, and it's easy to say in sync with a breathing exercise as a way of involving your body in the prayer. Breathe in while you're praying the first line of the prayer, and breathe out while you're praying the second line.

✤ Remember to thank God. How would you like it if you gave your child everything imaginable, but all you heard were requests for more. That's probably how it seems to God sometimes. Instead of asking (or demanding) things, thank God for what you've already been given. In fact, try writing down everything you want from God on a piece of paper. Then ball up the paper and throw it away—or if you have a candle where you pray, burn it. Get rid of your own agenda, and make prayer a time when you can learn God's agenda.

✤ Pray without ceasing. You may not be able to drop everything and go to the wilderness for forty days of prayer and fasting like Francis, but you can say a brief prayer when you first wake up in the morning, while you shower and get dressed, while you drive during the day, and when you lay your head on your pillow at night.

✤ One of the things I really like about Franciscan mysticism is the balance between mind and heart, between knowing about God and knowing God. Continue learning and studying about God's nature, and use what you learn as a grid through which you evaluate the things you receive in prayer. My own books, *The Lover and the Beloved* and *The Fire of God*, can tell you much more about what saints through the ages have said about communing with God, a subject that has inspired thousands of writers.

✤ Practice the disciplines of prayer. Prayer, like marriage, is a relationship that requires discipline and work. Don't expect to get very far in either marriage or prayer if all you want is the warm fuzzies. Feelings come and go, but love endures forever. Learn to endure in prayer and develop an evermore intimate relationship with God.

✤ Pray with others. Communion with God isn't a solo performance. For centuries, people of faith—both inside monasteries and out—have sought the encouragement and sustenance that comes from brothers and sisters praying alongside them. Many churches, retreat centers, and neighborhood groups offer opportunities to pray together with others. Seek out one of these groups.

✤ Take advantage of aids to prayer. Over the centuries, many believers have discovered tools that have helped them pray. Often people use a set of beads to keep track of the prayers. The Rosary is a recitation of fifteen sets of Hail Marys, each introduced by the Lord's Prayer and concluded with the Doxology. Much older is the practice of praying the Stations of the Cross, which represent fourteen scenes of Christ's passion. Perhaps you're near a church or retreat center with paintings or sculptures of the Stations of the Cross, an ancient practice that began with early pilgrims retracing the actual footsteps of Christ before his Crucifixion.

✤ Finally, jump in. But don't be afraid. The water really is fine. You may need to start by sticking in your toe, but my prayer is that over time, you will submerge yourself in God's deep, deep love.

society's poorest and most hopeless souls. Instead of marriage and family, he chose a life of celibacy, and his children were the untold thousands who have followed in his footsteps. Instead of going to France for commerce, he traveled throughout Europe to preach his radical and desperately needed message of penance and reform. And instead of having a pew or a plaque in one church, he now has thousands of churches, hospitals, and religious organizations dedicated to his honor.

But the people of Assisi had no idea of the great things in store for Francis. All they knew was that his life had been thrown violently off course. And in the opinion of some, he had strayed, becoming a primitive madman.

We know better. Through a heavenly convergence of good fortune, timing, geography, and divine intervention, Francis's life was transformed. Instead of being only vaguely remembered as an inconsequential footnote to the commercial history of a small medieval Italian town, Francis became the founder of a worldwide movement numbering more than a million. In fact, Franciscans make up the largest of the Catholic Church's many religious families. And for untold millions, Francis remains a potent reminder of what devotion to God looks like.

Hundreds of books explore the life of Francis and describe his impact. I feel like a midget standing on the shoulders of giants, and I share the frustration of Francis's first biographer, Thomas of Celano, who wrote: "It would take too long and it would be impossible to enumerate and gather together all the things the glorious Francis did and taught while he was living in the flesh."

Be that as it may, let's do the best we can to summarize the highlights of this remarkable and singular man in a few pages.

✣   ✣   ✣

The father of Francis, Pietro di Bernardone, was a big, boisterous businessman who hurriedly climbed the ladder of success as one of the members of a brand-new class of European capitalists. He made his money by buying low and selling high, traveling regularly to France to purchase luxurious cloth at discount rates and importing it to his shop in Assisi, where he made a healthy profit.

Pietro was conducting business in France in 1181 or 1182 (no one's sure of the exact date) when his wife Pica gave birth to a son who was baptized with the name Giovanni. Returning home, Pietro immediately changed his son's name to Francis, thus paying tribute to the family's growing reliance on their French connections.

While in his teens, Francis was made a junior partner in the family business. And after working with his father during the days, he would spend evenings with his friends drinking, carousing, and singing. "Almost up to the twenty-fifth year . . . he squandered and wasted his time miserably," wrote one biographer, who described the youthful Francis as "vain and proud" and said his friends unanimously selected him as "the master of revels."

Motivated by patriotic duty as well as the opportunity to gain even greater glory, Francis enlisted in Assisi's war against the neighboring town of Perugia around his twentieth year. But before he could engage the enemy, he was captured and put in prison, where he stayed for most of a year—his captors waiting until Francis's father would retrieve him with a lucrative ransom.

The following year Francis set out again for battle, this time in the service of a big-league papal army. But on the way to war, he had a vision that caused him to turn around and return home ill and disoriented. During a lengthy convalescence, Francis began losing his taste for the world of business, which worried his father, and became increasingly hungry for spiritual things, which intrigued his mother.

Believing that God wanted him to do something, but not knowing for sure what it was, he stopped in a small, run-down chapel to seek guidance. After a period of prayer and meditation, Francis heard the voice of Jesus coming from a nearby crucifix: "Francis, go, repair my house, which, as you see, is falling completely to ruin." Francis immediately dropped everything—and frankly, he didn't have much to drop—and began begging for stones and rebuilding the chapel. (It took a few more years and two more rebuilt churches before Francis began to get the idea that Jesus might want him to quit the construction trade and begin preaching.)

Seeing Francis begging in the streets, the people of Assisi cursed him, mocked him, and called him crazy. Women who once dreamed of marrying him now ran from him in horror. All of this gave Pietro no end of frustration and shame. But things soon got worse between father and son. Francis took some of his father's expensive cloth and sold it for building materials. Pietro tracked Francis down, captured him, and confined him to a cramped compartment in the family home, where he stayed for nearly a month until his father left on business and his mother let him go.

The conflict between Pietro and Francis culminated in

the father dragging the son before the local bishop in the hopes that the town's religious authority could talk some sense into the young man. But the plan backfired. There in front of God and everybody, Francis stripped off his clothing and handed it to his father. Standing there naked as the day he was born, Francis said, "Until now I called you my father, but from now on I can say without reserve, 'Our father who art in heaven.'"

Francis's father carried his son's clothes back to a large house that was now strangely quiet. Francis, on the other hand, went on his way rejoicing, suddenly freed from the encumbrances of wealth, family, and social esteem.

With time on his hands and God on his mind, Francis devoted himself to prayer. But one final barrier was left to cross before he could serve God with his whole heart. One day as he was walking down the road and saw a leper approaching him, he knew his opportunity was at hand. Francis wasn't alone in his discomfort with lepers, but he seemed to find them even more distasteful than most did. One biographer said he "naturally abhorred" them. But this day, when the leper approached Francis and held out his hand for a coin, Francis reached out and kissed him.

Francis didn't perform some incantation and immediately feel full of love for lepers. But by allowing God to love them through him, he opened up channels of spiritual energy that coursed through him with life-transforming force. Francis began hanging around with lepers, living in their communities, caring for them, and nursing their sores.

Attending Mass one day, Francis heard a priest read three passages from the Gospels he didn't recall having heard before. In one, Jesus tells a rich man who wanted to follow him, "Go, sell your possessions and give to the poor, and you will have treasure in heaven." In the second, Jesus sends out his twelve apostles to minister with these words: "Do not take along any gold or silver or copper in your belts; take no bag for the journey, or extra tunic, or sandals or a staff." In the third, Jesus says, "Anyone who does not take his cross and follow me is not worthy of me." Initially, these words stunned Francis into silence. Then they inflamed him to preach this message to anyone who would listen (and some who wouldn't).

Perhaps not surprisingly, word began to spread about Francis's selfless service to the lepers and his sermons about poverty and the cross. Before he knew it, Francis had a handful of followers, including the brothers Bernard and Peter Catanii who, like Francis, came from one of Assisi's better families. Unfortunately, none of the saint's sermons have survived the centuries. But St. Bonaventure remarks of the power of his words: "A person would certainly have to be really perverse and obstinate to refuse to listen to St. Francis's preaching."

Where first there were brothers Bernard and Peter following Francis, soon there were twelve. Feeling that he might have the beginnings of a movement on his hands, Francis slapped together some of his favorite Gospel passages, called the collection his first Rule, and went off to Rome to meet the pope. Like many religious leaders of the day, the pope was impressed by Francis's sincerity but perplexed by his insistence on such a literal application of the message of Jesus. Regardless, he welcomed Francis and his ragtag band and gave his tentative approval to their primitive Rule, which has been lost to history.

Like Jesus, Francis divided his twelve friars up and sent them out into the countryside two by two to preach. Soon there were a thousand. Then five thousand. All would gather once a year for joyous assemblies. Then they would divide up in twos again and be sent to farther reaches of the world, including Europe and Asia.

Francis's simple but radical message took shape at a time when everyone could see that the church was woefully off track. Or as Thomas of Celano put it: "When the teachings of the Gospel, not indeed in every respect, but taken generally, had everywhere failed to be put into practice, this man was sent by God to bear witness to the truth throughout the whole world."

Within five years of Francis's encounter with the crucifix, two other important things happened to his burgeoning fellowship of friars. Clare, the daughter of an aristocratic family, became the first woman to join the movement, founding the Poor Clares, a mystical order devoted to solitude and prayer. At about the same time, Francis began working with groups of devout laypeople. From these groups came the "secular" Franciscans of the Third Order, which was open to people who had families and jobs but still wanted to follow Francis's example.

With the movement growing rapidly, tensions cropped up that had not been evident when the group was smaller and closer. Specifically, arguments broke out over whether or not Franciscans should be held to the strict observance of poverty, with its ban on personal and corporate possessions. Eventually, the moderates won out, and Francis's rigid rules were relaxed, to the utter disgust of many of the more conservative brothers, some of whom were quite extreme and were later branded as heretics.

▨ A Living Legacy

When Francis died in 1226 at the age of forty-five, the fight over the issue of poverty was far from settled. Scholars still argue over what Francis really thought about the direction the order took. But in death as in life, he took the way of poverty. When near death, he didn't choose luxurious grave clothes. Instead, "he had himself placed naked upon the naked ground."

Francis was formally canonized as a saint by the Catholic Church at an event St. Bonaventure states was "a long ceremony which it would be tedious to describe." Today there are hundreds of officially recognized saints, but none has been so universally adored as Francis, a man historian Sir Kenneth Clark called "a religious genius—the greatest, I believe, that Europe has ever produced." Clark and others refer, no doubt, to Francis's tremendous impact on a troubled church in the centuries before the Protestant Reformation, as well as his immense influence on European art and culture in the years leading up to the Renaissance. But such accolades make Francis sound unbearably stuffy. .

I prefer the way a writer for *Look* magazine called Francis "a bearded, barefoot, slightly prankish, and largely unfathomable man." But that makes Francis sound slightly goofy. Maybe G. K. Chesterton put it best: "St. Francis walked the world like the Pardon of God."

Thomas à Kempis, a Dutch monk who lived a century after Francis, wrote a little book that became a masterpiece of medieval spirituality. His *The Imitation of Christ* could have served nicely as the title of a book about the life of Francis. "Francis sought not only to follow the words of Christ," wrote one biographer, "he wished also to imitate the life of Christ as perfectly as he could, and he willed that his friars too should 'follow the footsteps of our Lord Jesus Christ.' "

When one of the Franciscan brothers once asked the saint his preference in a certain matter, Francis's response was clear and sure: "That has always been and still is most dear to me and more sweet and more acceptable which pleases the Lord my God most to let happen in me and with me."

Years later, the authors of one of the most popular books about the saint, *The Little Flowers of St. Francis,* recounted a brother's vision, which powerfully describes Francis's desire to imitate Christ: "One night when Blessed Peter Pettinaio of the Third Order was praying in the Cathedral of Siena, he saw Our Lord Jesus Christ enter the church, followed by a great throng of saints. And each time Christ raised his foot, the form of his foot remained imprinted on the ground. And all the saints tried as hard as they could to place their feet in the traces of His footsteps, but none of them was able to do so perfectly. Then St. Francis came in and set his feet right in the footsteps of Jesus Christ."

Following God has never been easy. In times like ours it can seem downright baffling. But Francis gave it his best shot, and today his example continues to inspire many people who are strangely moved by the life of this unique and universal saint.

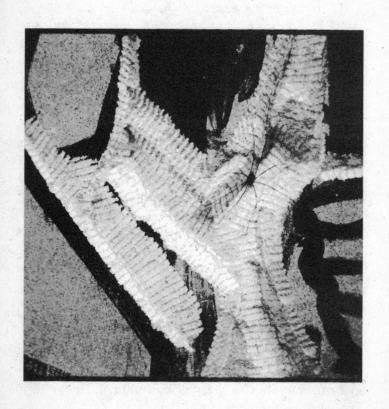

Notes

❦

🀫 A note on sources and information

Thank you for reading this book. I hope you found it helpful.

I would like to express my appreciation for two people who made this book possible. Scott Waxman of The Literary Group caught the vision and opened the doors. And Deirdre Mullane edited the project with an affection and skill that went way beyond the call of duty.

If you would like to know more about the life and teaching of Francis, here are some resources I recommend, and used in writing this book.

Francis: The Journey and the Dream, by Franciscan priest Murray Bodo (St. Anthony Messenger Press, 1988), was the first book I ever read about Francis, and it remains one of my favorites. Brief, accessible, and lyrical, the book is an excellent introduction to the saint.

At 1,665 pages and weighing in at three pounds, *St. Francis of Assisi: Omnibus of Sources of the Life of St. Francis*, edited by Marion Habig (Franciscan Press, 1991), is the mother of all Franciscan books. Included here are the writings of Francis, the biographies by Thomas of Celano and St. Bonaventure, *The Little Flowers*, and other important documents. All of the quotations from Francis and his biographers used in this book were taken from the *Omnibus*.

Franco Zeffirelli's 1973 film, *Brother Sun, Sister Moon*, remains the best movie about Francis, even if it (along with its soundtrack by Donovan) is a bit dated.

I also consulted the following books on Francis and his influence: *St. Francis of Assisi* by G. K. Chesterton (Doubleday & Company, 1987); *The Ideals of St. Francis of Assisi* by Hilarin Felder (Franciscan Press, 1983); *The Francis Book* compiled by Roy M. Gasnick (Collier, 1980); *A Short History of the Franciscan Family* by Damien Vorreux and Aaron Pembleton (Franciscan Press, 1989); and *The Franciscans: Love at Work* by Boniface Hanley and Salvator Fink (St. Anthony Guild Press, 1962).

I borrowed material from three of my previous books: *The Lover and the Beloved: A Way of Franciscan Prayer* (Troubador for the Lord, 1994); *Simplicity*, written with Dan O'Neill (Servant, 1989); and *The Master Musician: Meditations on Jesus* (Zondervan, 1992). These and other books are available by writing Little Portion Hermitage (address below).

In 1982 I recorded an album entitled *Troubadour of the Great King*, which consists of musical versions of the favorite scriptures and prayers of Francis. This and other albums are also available by writing Little Portion Hermitage.

▦ About the Little Portion Hermitage

Founded in 1980 and located outside of Eureka Springs, Arkansas, Little Portion is the monastic mother-house of the Brothers and Sisters of Charity, a Franciscan-based community including celibates, families, and singles, and supporting a network of people living in their own homes in America and five other countries. If you would like more information, please request our brochure, which describes our community and values.

We also run a conference center, Little Portion Retreat & Training Center at MORE Mountain, which offers regular retreats and workshops on contemplative prayer, simple living, monastic traditions, mystical prayer, and other subjects. Contact us if you're interested in videos or tapes from past conferences, or for a schedule of upcoming events.

We also publish a newsletter that includes news and information about our community and schedules of upcoming events at our conference center, as well as a schedule of my performances around the country, information on ordering books and music, a list of products made here at Little Portion and sold to support our ministries, and articles of interest. We would be glad to add you to our mailing list.

You can contact us by the following means:

✦ You can write us at: Route 7, Box 608, Eureka Springs, AR 72632
✦ You can phone us at: (501) 253-7710
✦ You can e-mail us at: bsCharity@aol.com
✦ Or you can visit our home page at the following Internet address: http:www.john-michael-talbot.org